THE TRUTH IS

ALL WE CAN AND NEED TO KNOW ABOUT GOD

RICHARD R. SCHAEFER

IBSN-13: 978-0-9909772-0-9

To Sandy, bride of my youth,

companion in all things,

love of my life

Did'ja ever sit and ponder, sit and wonder, sit and think,
Why we're here and what this life is all about?
It's a problem that has driven many brainy men to drink.
It's the weirdest thing they've tried to figure out.
About a thousand different theories, the scientists can
show.
But never yet have proved a reason why.
    . . .
Young for a day, then old and gray.
Like the rose that buds and blooms, and fades and falls
away.
Losing health in search of wealth, as through this dream
we tour.
Everything's a guess and nothing's absolutely sure.
Battles exciting, fates we're fighting, until the curtains
fall.
Life's a very funny proposition after all."

"Life's a Funny Proposition, After All," *Little Johnny Jones* by
George M. Cohan; transcribed from audio recording, *The
Smithsonian Collection of American Musical Theater*. 1990.

Contents

Preface

The Truth Is presents the results of my personal quest for an understanding of what Jesus' life was actually about. My quest began in a religious context - or, perhaps I should say, on the edge of a religious context. A lapsed Episcopalian at the time, I sensed that Jesus had been onto something, but I wasn't sure what that something was. While I was often moved by stories about Jesus in the New Testament, the meaning of Jesus' life, as it is represented in orthodox Christian creeds and doctrine, struck me as both implausible and arbitrary.

Throughout the busy years of pursuing my career (applied physics), helping to raise our sons, and pursuing an active social life, the notion that Jesus' life was about something more plausible and interesting than had been generally recognized, and warranted looking into, stayed with me. And so, when the chance presented itself, I returned to school to determine for myself what Jesus' life had been about. I applied to the Theology Department of the University of San Francisco, and was received by Father Egan, the department chairman, like a prodigal son. After five years of part-time study, including one year at the Yale Divinity School, I graduated with a Master of Arts degree in theology from USF, an ability to read biblical era Greek, and a familiarity with a variety of theological points of view and source material.

What could I do now with my education? I was not ministerial material; as I told my friends, I hadn't gone to school to become a good person, but rather to understand Jesus. And I wasn't interested in teaching; what would I have taught at this stage? My project was to discover what Jesus' life had been about. Fortunately, what Jesus' life was about is stated explicitly in the New Testament gospels. In the Gospel of John, Jesus declares, *"For this I was born, and for this I came into the world, to testify to the truth."* (John 18:37). In the other three gospels (Matthew, Mark, and Luke), Jesus uses somewhat different words to say essentially the same thing. In the Gospel of Luke, Jesus says that he has been anointed (designated by God) to preach good news: *"The Spirit of the Lord is upon me, because he has anointed me to preach good news to the poor. ..."* (Luke 4:18). Jesus had come to tell us something. And so, to know what Jesus' life was about I would need to know what he was trying to tell us.

I began my quest for the truth/good news by looking first in the Gospel of John. I did this for a number of reasons. First, John's Gospel is the source in which Jesus' purpose was most clearly stated. Second, it is the only Gospel that claims to have been written (with the exception of some comments by a final editor) by an eyewitness to Jesus' ministry. Third, John's Gospel places Jesus' life in a larger, cosmic and spiritual context, and that intrigued me. And, fourth, I hadn't spent much time with the Gospel of John while in school, so it represented more of a challenge.

Early on, I realized that the Gospel of John is so rich in thought and language that there would not be time or space for me to also address the other Gospels - and do them justice in one book. And so, the object of my quest became the truth to which Jesus testified *as it is represented in the Gospel of John*. What was to have been just a chapter now became the book.

It might seem that this reduction in scope of my quest for the truth would limit the scope of the findings. But this is not the case. The truth to which Jesus testifies in the Gospel of John transcends its immediate context and fully addresses the fundamental questions about our lives and about existence in its entirety. Is existence about something, or nothing? Is there a purpose behind existence? And, will anything we do or fail to do in this life have mattered, when all is said and done?

Although I have found the truth to which Jesus testified in what is generally considered to be a Christian document, the truth as represented in the Gospel of John is not particularly Christian. It is universal - applicable to, and accessible by, anyone, whatever their religious affiliation, or lack thereof. The focus of the truth is not on Jesus, but rather on four questions: who (or what) is God, who are we, what we are meant to be doing, and what is salvation? The answers contained in the truth are "nondenominational" in the broadest sense. Within any religious context the truth could - and I believe should - be adopted as the basis for understanding, interpreting, and prioritizing among the numerous - often mutually incompatible - beliefs that have accumulated over time. For the non-religious, the truth provides an alternative to traditional religion for ordering one's life, and a basis for knowing what matters and what doesn't.

I frequently quote passages from the Gospel of John in this book, but not as evidence that what they say is true. I quote them only to establish that what I am claiming is said in the Gospel *is* actually said in the Gospel. Whether we recognize that what is said is true, or not, is up to us.

I have endeavored to carry out my analysis of the Gospel of John in an orderly and transparent manner so as to facilitate the reader's understanding of the truth. This book may not be a fast read. However, if you are willing to ponder things at your own pace, I believe it will be rewarding. And, inasmuch as you have gotten this far, I believe you have it in you.

Chapter 1

IS EXISTENCE ABOUT SOMETHING?

Now and then, during our busy and complicated lives, a certain question might occur to us, a question having to do with existence in its entirety, and our individual lives in particular. The question could be put this way: is existence about something, or nothing? And if existence *is* about something, what is that something?

The question may then slip from our consciousness, but it is likely to return. We might choose to put the question differently. We might ask ourselves, is there a purpose behind existence? And, if so, what is that purpose? Or, we might ask ourselves whether anything we do, or fail to do, will have mattered when all is said and done. And, if something will have mattered, what is that something?

How we choose to put the question is not as important as the answer we give ourselves and others. Our answer will influence everything that we think and do going forward. The answer is, from a certain perspective, a matter of life and death.

What is the truth about existence? Is there even such a thing as "the truth" about existence? I believe that there is and, moreover, that it is possible for us to know the truth. But, unfortunately, the truth is often misunderstood or misrepresented. It has become fashionable in some circles to deny the existence of any such thing as "the truth" in an objective sense, and to doubt that we could know the truth if it there were one. Consequently, it is not surprising that many of us are uncertain about existence, about the purpose behind existence, and about what matters and what doesn't.

Some of us avoid the question because we fear that existence might *not* be about anything, that there might *not* be any purpose behind existence, and that nothing we do or fail to do will have mattered. This is how a prominent writer, Jose Saramago, has characterized our situation:

> *This often happens, we refrain from asking a question because we are unprepared or simply too afraid to hear the answer. And when finally we summon the courage to ask, no answer is forthcoming, just as Jesus one day will refuse to answer when asked, What is truth. A question that remains unanswered to this day.*[1]

Fortunately for us, Mr. Saramago is mistaken. The question, "What is truth?," does not remain unanswered. Moreover, the answer can be found in a text that is readily accessible to all: the Gospel of John - precisely the text to which Mr. Saramago alludes. His statement that "Jesus

---

[1] Jose Saramago, *The Gospel According to Jesus Christ,* translated by Giovanni Pontiero, Houghton Mifflin Harcourt, 1994. (Quote from page 557 of the Quality Paperback Edition, 1999).

one day will refuse to answer when asked, What is truth?," is somewhat misleading. It is true that Jesus does not answer Pilate when asked, What is truth? However, Jesus doesn't answer because Pilate isn't really interested in an answer. Pilate's question is rhetorical, dismissive of "truth" as a topic worthy of discussion. Without waiting for an answer, Pilate turns and leaves the room. In his dismissal of the truth, he adopts a "post-modern" position - ages before the advent of modernity itself.

Jesus does not answer Pilate in the Gospel; however, he does reveal the truth to others throughout the Gospel of John. All we need to do in order to uncover the truth - as it was understood by the author of the Gospel, and by Jesus as he is represented in the Gospel - is to pay close attention to the text of the Gospel, particularly to the words attributed to Jesus and to the comments of the author.

Although the Gospel of John is one of the early Christian writings that were selected for inclusion in the New Testament, the truth, as it is represented in Gospel, is not particularly Christian. That is to say, the truth represented in the text does not call for any belief about Jesus *other than* that the truth to which he testified is true and, moreover, the decisive truth about our lives.

My purpose in writing this book has been to determine, and to express as clearly as I can, the truth to which Jesus testified - as it is represented in the Gospel of John. My hope is that, in so doing, I will contribute to making the truth more accessible to others, in particular to those who sense that existence *is* about something, that there *is* a purpose behind existence, and that what we do in this life *does* matter. Before we proceed with our search for the truth, I believe it will be helpful to begin with a brief overview of the Gospel of John.

Overview of the Gospel

The Gospel of John is a narrative representation of the last few years in the life of Jesus - a person living, as we do, in a time of widespread misunderstanding and misrepresentation of the truth. Jesus had come to know the truth, and he recognized that it offered us freedom: freedom from slavery to the things of this world (*Then Jesus said, . . . "If you continue in my word, you are truly my disciples; and you will know the truth, and the truth will make you free."* 8:31-32).[2]

Jesus also recognized his personal responsibility to testify to the truth, and that to do so was his reason for

---

[2] Quotes from the Gospel of John are indicated in italics and are taken from the New Revised Standard Version (NRSV) of the Bible, except in those few instances where I take exception to the NRSV translation (and/or to the underlying Greek). In those instances in which I diverge from the NRSV reading, I will acknowledge the divergence and explain my reasons for doing so. On occasion I will also mention and comment on other prominent translations, such as the King James Version (KJV) and the New International version (NIV). The numbers at the end of quotations from the Gospel, here and elsewhere in this work, correspond to the chapter and verses encompassed by the quote.

being (*"For this I was born, and for this I came into the world, to testify to the truth."* 18:37). Jesus understood that by testifying to the truth he would at the same time be revealing who he was, for the truth constituted his true being. And it would be by entering into Jesus' being - by accepting and abiding in the truth - that others would come to have "life," eternal life. Thus Jesus was able to claim, *"I am the way, and the truth, and the life."* (14:6).

Jesus recognized that the truth he was revealing was not his own, but rather had its origin in God, in the one who had sent him (*"My teaching is not mine but his who sent me."* 7:16). In his testimony Jesus was completely dependent upon God, whom he would refer to as his Father ("*... I do nothing on my own, but I speak these things as the Father instructed me."* 8:28) and as the Father of all those who would come to know and embody the truth. Jesus recognized that he (himself) was not the Father ("*. . . the Father is greater than I."* 14:28) but saw himself as one *with* the Father ("*The Father and I are one."* 10:30).

In presenting his testimony to the truth, Jesus spoke openly (*"I have spoken openly to the world; I have always taught in synagogues and in the temple ... I have said nothing in secret."* (18:20). But he often employed figures of speech, metaphor (*"I am the bread of life ..."* 6:35) and riddle (*"A little while, and you will no longer see me, and again a little while and you will see me."* 16:16).

5

Is Existence About Something?

Jesus' words were accepted by some (*When they heard these words, some in the crowd said, "This is really the prophet." Others said, "This is the Messiah."* 7:40-41a), but others were puzzled (*The Jews then disputed among themselves, saying, "How can this man give us his flesh to eat?"* (6:52) and *"What does he mean by saying to us, 'A little while, and you will no longer see me, and again a little while and you will see me'...?* (16:17)). Even some among his disciples found his words difficult to accept (*When many of his disciples heard it, they said, "This teaching is difficult; who can accept it?"* 6:60), and many turned away from him (*Because of this many of his disciples turned back and no longer went about with him.* 6:66). Some felt that he was attempting to make himself God; and so they took up stones in order to kill him (*"It is not for a good work that we are going to stone you, but for blasphemy, because you, though only a human being, are making yourself God."* 10:33).

In spite of this opposition, Jesus' influence continued to grow, so much so that the religious authorities became alarmed: *So the chief priests and the Pharisees called a meeting of the council, and said, "What are we to do? ... If we let him go on like this, everyone will believe in him, and the Romans will come and destroy both our holy place and our nation."* (11:47-48). A solution to this problem was then suggested by Caiaphas, the high priest: *"... it is better that one man die for the people than to have the whole nation destroyed."* (11:50). And from that day forward the religious authorities plotted Jesus' death.

Jesus was eventually arrested, turned over to the Roman authorities on charges of claiming to be the king of the Jews (*Pilate also had an inscription written and put on the cross. It read, "Jesus of Nazareth, the King of the Jews."* 19:19), and put to death.

The narrative portion of John's Gospel does not end with Jesus' death. After a few days Jesus reappears, first to Mary Magdalene, and then to others of his disciples. In these appearances, Jesus offers the disciples some final words of encouragement and instruction: *Jesus said to them again, "Peace be with you. As the Father sent me I send you." (20:21).*

The text ends with the words of a final editor (or editors) - words which tell us that the Gospel had originally been written by one of Jesus' disciples, a person identified only as "the disciple whom Jesus loved." The editor then adds his and his colleagues' testimony to the truthfulness of "the beloved disciple's" account, saying, *This is the person who is testifying to these things and has written them, and we know that his testimony is true. (21:24).*

This brief overview of the Gospel of John highlights the centrality of "the truth," both to the Gospel and to Jesus' life as it was understood by the author of the Gospel. In verse 18:37 Jesus tells Pilate that his purpose was to testify to the truth. Was this Jesus' purpose?

Jesus' Purpose

The understanding that Jesus' purpose was to testify
to the truth is consistent with, and strongly supported by,
what we find Jesus saying and doing throughout the
Gospel. It is consistent with the representation of Jesus'
life in what is often spoken of as the prologue of the
Gospel (verses 1:1-18). It is also consistent with what we
find Jesus doing throughout the main narrative. And it is
consistent with what Jesus, as his death draws near,
claims to have accomplished.

In the prologue of the Gospel, even before he has been
identified by name, Jesus is represented as one coming
into the world to enlighten mankind (*The true light, which
enlightens everyone, was coming into the world.* 1:9).
Then, only a few verses later, the author declares that
Jesus had embodied "the Word" (the author's term for
what Jesus refers to as "the truth"): *And the Word became
flesh and lived among us ...* (1:14). The author then goes
on to state that, while Moses brought the law, Jesus
brought grace and truth (*The law indeed was given by
Moses; grace and truth came through Jesus Christ.* 1:16).
Finally, the prologue concludes by saying that Jesus had
made God known (*No one has ever seen God. It is the
only Son, who is close to the Father's heart, who has
made him known.*[3] (1:18). Thus, the prologue prepares us

---

[3] Here (and from here on) I take exception to the NRSV translation of
verse 1:18. The second sentence in the NRSV reads: "It is God the
only Son who ...." The extraneous "God" appears to have been

for a story about a person who came into this world to enlighten mankind, to reveal the truth, and to make God known. Throughout the Gospel everything we find Jesus doing is consistent with the understanding that his purpose had been to testify to the truth. We find Jesus teaching:

... Jesus went up to the temple and began to teach. The Jews were astonished at it, saying, "How does this man have such learning, when he has never been taught?" Then Jesus answered them, "My teaching is not mine but his who sent me. Anyone who resolves to do the will of God will know whether the teaching is from God or whether I am speaking on my own." (7:14-17), and

"You call me Teacher and Lord -- and you are right, for that is what I am." (13:13).

We find him speaking:

"... The words that I say to you I do not speak on my own; but the Father who dwells in me does his works." (14:10), and

---

inserted in some copies of the Gospel at some point, perhaps to advance a theological point of view. See *The Orthodox Corruption of Scripture*, by Bart Ehrman. No ancient Greek manuscript actually contains (in translation) "God the only Son." See, New Testament Greek Manuscripts: John, edited by Reuben J. Swanson, William Carey International University Press, Pasadena, CA. 1995.

Jesus answered, "I have spoken openly to the world; I have always taught in synagogues and in the temple, where all the Jews come together. I have said nothing in secret." (18:20).

And we find him emphasizing what he is saying by introducing his words with "Very truly" (or in some other translations, "Amen, Amen"):

"Very truly, I tell you, anyone who hears my words and believes him who sent me has eternal life, and does not come under judgment, but has passed from death to life." (5:24).

Jesus teaches, speaks in public, and emphasizes the importance of his words throughout John's Gospel. He is also represented in the Gospel as performing impressive acts, such as feeding a multitude with only a few loaves of bread and fish, restoring sight to a man born blind, and raising a man (Lazarus) from the dead. But these and similar stories are really just figurative representations of his testifying to the truth, and of the effect of his words on those who receive them - as we shall see.

Finally, as his death draws near, Jesus tells the Father, *"I have made your name known to those whom you gave me from the world. ... Now they know that everything you have given me is from you; for the words that you gave to me I have given to them, and they have received them ..."* (17:6-8), and, *"I have given them your word ..."* (17:14).

It is clear - from the prologue, from what Jesus says he came into the world to do, from what we find him doing throughout the Gospel, and from what he claims to have accomplished - that Jesus understood that his purpose was to testify to the truth.

Jesus also speaks of having come into this world to do the will of God ("*... I have come down from heaven, not to do my own will, but the will of him who sent me.*" 6:38). He then goes on to say that it is the will of God that those who see the Son may have eternal life and be raised up (*"This indeed is the will of my Father, that all who see the Son and believe in him may have eternal life; and I will raise them up on the last day."* 6:40).

The understanding that Jesus had come to do God's will is fully compatible with the understanding that he had come to testify to the truth. It was by testifying to the truth that Jesus did God's will. And it was by testifying to the truth that Jesus empowered those who believed to have eternal life.

On other occasions, Jesus seems to be saying that he came to judge the world (*Jesus said, "I came into this world for judgment, so that those who do not see may see, and those who do see may become blind."* 9:39). But judgment was not Jesus' purpose; rather, it was a natural consequence of his testimony. Jesus' words (the words given to him by the Father) have the effect of enabling those who "do not see" (those who do not yet understand and recognize the truth) to see. At the same time, his words reveal that those who "do see" (those who have falsely claimed to see) had been blind to the truth all along.

Jesus himself did *not* come to judge us or anyone - but judgment does occur. As he explains later in the Gospel,

> *"I do not judge anyone who hears my words and does not keep them, for I came not to judge the world, but to save the world. The one who rejects me and does not receive my word has a judge; on the last day the word that I have spoken will serve as judge."* (12:47-48)

The *word* that Jesus had spoken, the *truth* to which he testified, is our judge. Jesus makes it clear in this passage that he came *not* to judge, but rather to save the world. "To save the world" is *a* purpose behind what Jesus does, and it is *a* purpose behind God's having sent Jesus to testify.

Jesus came to testify to the truth and, in so doing, he enabled us to have life (eternal life). He anticipated that he would be killed ("lifted up" on the cross) for his efforts: ... *Jesus said, "When you have lifted up the Son of Man, then you will realize that I am he, and that I do nothing on my own, but I speak these things as the Father instructed me."* (8:28). But he continued to testify, and his willingness to die to make the truth known was itself part of his testimony.

Eternal life and salvation could not (and cannot) be imposed on the world. The world could be saved only by making the truth known, and this is the task that Jesus took upon himself. Jesus testified to the truth, and the rest was/is up to us.

In my brief overview of the Gospel I claimed that Jesus, in testifying to the truth, would be revealing who he was; and I pointed out that Jesus had claimed to *be* the truth. Did Jesus really think of himself as being the truth? And, if so, what did he mean by saying so?

The Truth *as* Jesus

Jesus identifies himself as "the truth" directly only in verse 14:6 of the Gospel (*"I am the way, the truth, and the life."*), but he often does so indirectly, employing metaphorical language. Some particularly relevant passages in the Gospel employ "bread" as a metaphor - first for the truth, or the word of God, and then for Jesus himself. These passages reveal Jesus' understanding of his identity, and they also provide the key for understanding some of his more enigmatic sayings in the Gospel.

The "bread passages" appear, for the most part, in chapter six of the Gospel. Bread is first mentioned in the story about the feeding a large crowd on a mountain by the Sea of Galilee (verses 6:1-14). On the surface, this story appears to be about a miracle performed by Jesus.

The miracle in this case is that Jesus is somehow able to feed five thousand people with only five loaves of bread and two fish. Everyone is satisfied, and yet enough fragments are left over to fill twelve baskets!

> *Then Jesus took the loaves, and when he had given thanks, he distributed them to those who were seated; so also the fish, as much as they wanted. When they were satisfied, he told his disciples, "Gather up the fragments left over, so that nothing may be lost." So they gathered them up, and from the fragments of the five barley loaves left by those who had eaten, they filled twelve baskets. When the people saw the sign that he had done, they began to say, "This is indeed the prophet who is to come into the world."* (6:11-14).

However, if we take into account the context in which the story is embedded it becomes clear that the story is not about the feeding of a crowd with loaves and fish in the literal sense. Rather, the story is a figurative representation of Jesus' teaching, his speaking the word(s) of God, his testifying to the truth.

What reason is there to believe that the story of the feeding of the five thousand might be a figurative representation of Jesus teaching? The first reason has to do with the special meaning that is attached to the word "bread" in the Gospel. Bread most often serves as a metaphor for the word of God, that is, for the truth. And the metaphorical meaning of bread in this story is revealed shortly after the feeding story itself.

After the feeding of the five thousand, Jesus crosses the Sea of Galilee, and the crowd (the same crowd that has just been fed) follows and asks Jesus what sign he can give them, so that they might believe him. That the crowd is still seeking a sign is somewhat surprising inasmuch as they had earlier followed Jesus to the mountain where the feeding took place *because they saw the signs that he was doing* (6:2). They were also present at the feeding itself and had taken it to be a sign (*When they saw the sign he had done, they began to say, "This is indeed the prophet who is to come into the world." 6:14*). And they had also found Jesus inexplicably transported across the sea without a boat. Nevertheless, the crowd asks for a sign:

> So they said to him, *"What sign are you going to give us then, so that we may see it and believe you? What work are you performing? Our ancestors ate the manna in the wilderness; as it is written, 'He gave them bread from heaven to eat.'"* (6:30-31).

In his answer Jesus speaks of the "bread from heaven" and "the bread of God":

> Then Jesus said to them, *"Very truly, I tell you, it was not Moses who gave you the bread from heaven, but it is my Father who gives you the true*

bread from heaven. For the bread of God is that
which comes down from heaven and gives life to
the world. They said to him, "Sir, give us this
bread always." (6:32-34).

What is "the bread from heaven," "the true bread from heaven," "the bread of God" of which Jesus is speaks in this passage? We are told within the passage that it is that which "gives life to the world." And so we need to ask ourselves, what it is that comes down and gives life to the world? In the prologue to the Gospel, we are told that "the Word" brings life into being (*In the beginning was the Word ... All things came into being through it[4] ... What has come into being in it was life ...* 1:1-4). And in the body of the Gospel, Jesus refers to his own word (which, as we know from verse 7:16, is not actually his own, but God's) as bringing life, eternal life: *"Very truly, I tell you, anyone who hears my word and believes him who sent me has eternal life, and does not come under judgment, but has passed from death to life." (5:24).* Clearly, the bread of which Jesus speaks in chapter six is the Word, the word of God, the truth to which Jesus testified.

Further evidence to indicate that the story of the feeding of the five thousand might be about Jesus'

---

[4] Here, and throughout the present work, I translate the Greek pronouns in this passage as neuter (it) so as to best fit the noun (logos) to which they refer. Most translations render these pronouns as masculine (him) under the mistaken impression that they refer to Jesus, who has not yet been mentioned in the text.

teaching can be found within the feeding story itself. Early in the story, Jesus decides to put one of his disciples, Philip, to a test.

> *When he looked up and saw a large crowd coming toward him, Jesus said to Philip, "Where are we to buy bread for these people to eat?" He said this to test him, for he himself knew what he was going to do. Philip answered him, "Six months' wages would not buy enough bread for each of them to get a little." One of his disciples, Andrew, Simon Peter's brother, said to him, "There is a boy here who has five barley loaves and two fish. But what are they among so many people?"* (6:5-9).

What was the test to which Jesus put Philip? One possibility, and perhaps the most common understanding of this passage, is that Jesus was testing Philip's faith, his faith that he (Jesus) would somehow be able to satisfy the crowd's physical hunger with just a few loaves and fish. But another possibility -- and what I believe the author really had in mind -- is that Jesus was testing Philip to see if he understood that the bread he intended to give to the people was in fact the "bread" that comes down from heaven and gives life, i.e., the word of God. In this understanding of the story, Philip fails the test.

How are we to ascertain what the author (or Jesus) really had in mind regarding the test? Another clue - both to what the feeding story represents and to what the test

17

must have been - comes just after the feeding story has, or appears to have, ended. Jesus' disciples have crossed over the sea of Galilee, and the crowd has followed after them. They are puzzled to find Jesus on the other side, inasmuch as he had not gotten into the boat with his disciples. Here's what the Gospel tells us:

> *When they found him on the other side of the sea, they said to him, "Rabbi, when did you come here? Jesus answered them, "Very truly, I tell you, you are looking for me, not because you saw signs, but because you ate your fill of the loaves."* (6:25-26).

In this passage, Jesus does not respond directly to the crowds' question about *when* he had come to the other side of the sea. Instead he takes the opportunity to set the crowd straight (and the author takes the opportunity to set the reader straight) on all this "sign" business. Jesus tells them that they are following him not because of any signs, but rather because they have eaten their fill of the loaves, that is, because they have taken in the truth to which Jesus testified. This passage is a key to understanding not only the feeding story (and the test), but also to understanding much of what is said throughout the Gospel.

If the feeding story had been about a miraculous event in the conventional sense, the event would have *been* a sign. But in verses 6:25-26 Jesus is contrasting seeing signs with receiving metaphorical "loaves" of the truth.

He tells the crowd that they are looking for him not because of signs, but because of his words, because of his testimony to the truth.

If we understand the feeding of the five thousand as a story about Jesus' teaching, then the reference to twelve baskets of leftovers is also understandable. Since the loaves represent the words that Jesus has spoken to the crowd, it is not at all surprising that there is plenty to go around. The truth is not exhausted in the telling; there is enough left over to fill "twelve baskets," an expression that might have been understood by the early readers of John's Gospel to represent the twelve tribes that comprised the whole of ancient Israel.

A reading of the story of the feeding of the five thousand in both its immediate and larger contexts makes it clear that the "bread" of which Jesus speaks in the story, is the word of God, the truth to which he testified. We have been looking into the meaning of the story of the feeding of the five thousand in order to prepare ourselves for a further discussion of Jesus' identification with the truth. And so, we return to that discussion now.

In verses 6:30-34, after Jesus has set his listeners straight on the matter of loaves and signs, his listeners again ask him for a sign, and they mention that Moses gave them bread from heaven to eat. Jesus replies that it is God who gives the true bread from heaven that gives life to the world, and his listeners then ask Jesus, "Sir, give us this bread always." At this point Jesus first claims that he *is* the bread of life (*Jesus said to them, "I am the bread of life. Whoever comes to me will never be hungry, and whoever believes in me will never be thirsty."* 6:35). He then repeats and elaborates on this claim:

> *"I am the bread of life. Your ancestors ate the manna in the wilderness, and they died. This is the bread that comes down from heaven, so that one may eat of it and not die. I am the living bread that came down from heaven. Whoever eats of this bread will live forever; and the bread that I will give for the life of the world is my flesh."* (6:48-51).

In identifying himself *as* the "bread," Jesus is expressing in metaphor the same point that he makes in verse 14:6, in which he directly claimed identity with the truth.

What Did Jesus Mean?

What did Jesus mean in saying that he is the truth? Are we to understand that Jesus' material being, his physical self, somehow constituted the truth? Or is it that the truth somehow constituted Jesus' being? As a practical matter, do we come to know what the truth is by pursuing material facts about Jesus (apart from what he said)? Or, do we come to know who Jesus was (and is) by coming to know the truth to which he testified?

Actually, we can come to know Jesus, the essence of who he was and is, *only* by coming to know the truth to

which he testified. Jesus would not have been who he
was had he not said the things that he said. The truth to
which he testified constituted Jesus' essential being - not
his body, his material being, but his transcendent being.
As a result, there is no such thing as knowing Jesus
without knowing the truth to which he testified.

That it was Jesus' words - or rather the truth behind
his words - that constituted his being can be appreciated if
we consider another story in the Gospel of John: the story
of "the woman caught in adultery." Listen.

> *Early in the morning he came again to the temple.*
> *All the people came to him and he sat down and*
> *began to teach them. The scribes and the*
> *Pharisees brought a woman who had been caught*
> *in adultery; and making her stand before all of*
> *them, they said to him, "Teacher, this woman was*
> *caught in the very act of committing adultery.*
> *Now in the law Moses commanded us to stone*
> *such women. Now what do you say?" They said*
> *this to test him, so that they might have some*
> *charge to bring against him. ...* [7] *When they kept*
> *on questioning him, he straightened up and said to*
> *them, "Let anyone among you who is without sin*
> *be the first to throw a stone at her." ... When they*
> *heard it, they went away, one by one, beginning*
> *with the elders; and Jesus was left alone with the*
> *woman standing before him.* [10] *Jesus straightened*
> *up and said to her, "Woman, where are they? Has*
> *no one condemned you?"* [11] *She said, "No one,*

sir." And Jesus said, "Neither do I condemn you.
Go your way, and from now on do not sin again."
(8:2-11).

In his response to the question put to him by the
scribes and Pharisees, Jesus could not have said just
anything - and still have been who he was. He could not
have said, "Very truly, I tell you, we must stone this
woman in accordance with scripture" - and still have been
the person he was. Jesus' true self was constituted by the
truth to which he testified. The truth is that God does not
want us to kill one another at all, and certainly not in his
name. God does *not* condemn us. He wants us to love
and care for others whatever their guilt or innocence.

Jesus was constrained in what he could say by the
Word, by the truth to which he had come into this world
to testify. He could not have said just anything and still
have been worthy of the titles of respect that he is given in
the Gospel: the Messiah/Christ, the Son of God. What
Jesus said wasn't true *because* he said it. Rather, he said
it because it was true, and it had been true from the
beginning. What Jesus said wasn't true because he was
the Messiah, and Son of God. Rather, he can be thought
of as the Messiah, the Son of God, because what he was
saying was the truth.

In the prologue, the author tells us that, in Jesus, the
Word was made flesh (*And the Word was made flesh and*
lived among us ... 1:14). How are we to understand this
statement? Was the Word literally turned into flesh? Are

22

we to think of Jesus, that is, of his flesh, as *being* the Word? No. The Word did not *become* flesh in a literal sense. Why would it? After all, as Jesus points out, flesh is useless: *"It is the spirit that gives life; the flesh is useless."* (6:63) What the author actually meant in saying that "the Word was made flesh" is that the Word was *embodied* by Jesus -- much as the spirit of competition might come to be embodied by a football coach ("Winning isn't everything; it's the only thing"[5]). In a spiritual sense, winning isn't everything. It isn't anything. But that's another book.

The Word, although embodied by Jesus, did not cease being the Word. Nor did the Word "disappear" into Jesus. Rather, the Word continued being the Word - undiminished by having been embodied. In other words, God did not disappear into Jesus. Accordingly, God, the Father, remains a character distinct from Jesus throughout the Gospel of John. Jesus speaks of God (or, equivalently, of the Father) in the third person throughout the Gospel. He is careful to distinguish between himself and God, and to emphasize his dependence on God for what he is saying and doing:

Then Jesus answered them, "My teaching is not mine but his who sent me. Anyone who resolves to do the will of God will know whether the teaching

---

[5] According to *Bartlett's Familiar Quotations*, Seventeenth Edition, published by Little, Brown and Company in 2002, this saying is "often attributed to U.C.L.A. football coach Henry ("Red") Sanders."

is from God or whether I am speaking on my own.
(7:16-17),

*Jesus said to them, "Very truly, I tell you, the Son
can do nothing on his own, but only what he sees
the Father doing ...* (5:19), and

*"... I have not spoken on my own, but the Father
who sent me has himself given me a commandment
about what to say and what to speak. ... What I
speak, therefore, I speak just as the Father has
told me.* (12:49-50).

God remains God (and, equivalently, the Word
remains the Word) throughout the Gospel of John.

Not only are God and Jesus represented as distinct
beings in the Gospel of John, but Jesus makes it clear that
he is subordinate to God. As his arrest and execution
approaches, Jesus tells his disciples directly, *"... If you
loved me, you would rejoice that I am going to the Father,
because the Father is greater than I."* (14:28).

Problem Passages

In spite of the clear evidence to the contrary, there are
a few passages in the Gospel of John that could be
understood to be saying that Jesus was God, or
understood himself to be God. For instance, in the
prologue to the Gospel we find: *No one has ever seen
God. It is God the only Son, who is close to the Father's*

heart, who has made him known. (1:18). Was the author thinking that God was the only Son? Or that the only Son was God? In either case, the verse would appear to be saying that God is close to the Father's heart? But why would anyone say this? God *is* the Father! Moreover, the verse suggests that the only Son *is* God - a notion that is incompatible with the many passages in the Gospel that represent Jesus as being subordinate to God. Something appears to be wrong with the wording of the second sentence in verse 1:18 - either in the underlying Greek text or the translation (or both).

Some of the ancient manuscripts containing verse 1:18 read (when translated into English), "It is the only Son ..." Others read, "It is the only God ..." (and none of them read. "It is God the only Son ..."). The ancient manuscripts which read "It is the only Son ..." make the most sense because the truth to which Jesus testifies does concern the identity of God. At the same time, one could take exception to the word "only" - and I will do so in Chapter 7: Son of Man/Son of God.

The confusion concerning the wording of the Greek text of verse 1:18 appears to be caused by an alteration of the original Greek wording in some copies of the Gospel relatively early in the history of transmission of the Gospel.[6] The corrupted text ("It is the only God") was

---

[6] "...the majority of manuscripts are right in ending the prologue with the words, 'No one has seen God at any time, but the unique Son who is in the bosom of the Father, that one has made him known.'" The variant reading of the Alexandrian tradition which substitutes

then faithfully reproduced in one family of manuscripts, a family referred to by textual critics as the "Alexandrian tradition." It is this corrupted text that provides the basis for the New Revised Standard Version (NRSV) and some other translations of verse 1:18. The uncorrupted Greek text supports those translations that attribute the making of God known to the Son, and avoid suggesting that the Son is God, and that God is in the Father's bosom. For example, the King James Version (KJV) reads, *No man has seen God at any time; the only begotten Son which is in the Father, he hath declared him.* "). Thus verse 1:18 should not be viewed as supporting the notion that Jesus was or is God, or that the author believed Jesus to *be* God.

Another passage that might seem to indicate that Jesus was, or believed himself to be, God is his declaration in verse 10:30: *"The Father and I are one."* The question we need to ask here is, does being "one" with the Father mean *being* the Father? Does it in the Gospel of John? No. In order to understand verse 10:30 we need to take into account the ways Jesus speaks of being "one with someone or something" throughout the Gospel. Oneness with the Father is not an attribute exclusive to Jesus in the text. Late in the Gospel, just before he is arrested, Jesus

---

"God" for "Son," represents an orthodox corruption of the text in which the complete deity of Christ is confirmed ..." The Orthodox Corruption of Scripture: The Effect of Early Christological Controversies on the Text of the New Testament by Bart D. Ehrman, Oxford University Press, New York and Oxford, 1993, pp. 78-79.

prays to the Father on behalf of those who have believed, and those who *will* believe, in him:

> *"I ask not only on behalf of these, but also on behalf of those who will believe in me through their word, that they may all be one. As you, Father, are in me, and I am in you, may they also be in us, so that the world may believe that you have sent me. The glory that you have given me I have given them, so that they may be one, as we are one, I in them and you in me."* (17:20-23).

In John's Gospel, being one with the Father is a state of being in which the Father is *in* a person, and that person is *in* the Father. It is a condition which applies to Jesus ("As you, Father, are in me, and I am in you") and which can apply to others ("may they all be in us"). Thus Jesus' oneness with the Father is not unique ("... so that they may be one, as we are one, I in them and you in me."). It is a state of being enjoyed by all who come to believe, and to bring their lives into accord with, the truth.

In attempting to understand a text as complex as the Gospel of John is, there will often be problem passages, passages that do, or seem to, contradict a conclusion that we are inclined to draw. The overarching principle that should be applied in interpreting a text is that the interpretation should best take into account and represent what is said throughout the entire text. When a problem passage is encountered, it should be dealt with by: (a) explaining how the passage is actually consistent with the interpretation, (b) explaining why the passage can be ignored (for example, as a corruption of the original text, or as a mistranslation), (c) adjusting the interpretation so as to accommodate the problem passage, or (d) recognizing that the passage cannot be accommodated.

Reasonable Expectations

The Gospel of John is at best a secondary source of evidence regarding the truth to which Jesus testified. However, the Gospel is a *primary* source of evidence regarding its author's understanding of that truth.[7] By paying careful attention to the text of the Gospel, we should be able to develop our own understanding of the truth - as it was understood by the author. Having done so, we will be in a position to discover whether or not it strikes us as true and, moreover, the decisive truth about our own life.

Because the author represents his protagonist (Jesus) as stating that he had come into the world to testify to the truth, it is reasonable to expect to find a representation of the truth in his Gospel. Moreover, because the truth (the Word) is said to have brought "all things" - and, in particular, "life" - into being, we can expect this truth to be concerned with existence in its entirety, and our own lives in particular.

---

[7] Here I am assuming that the *representation* of the truth in the Gospel represents the Gospel's author's *understanding* of the truth to which Jesus testified.

28

Is Existence About Something?

In my pursuit of the truth in the Gospel of John, I have meant to: (1) let the text of the Gospel itself suggest the primary topic (the truth) and the subtopics and associated questions; (2) identify and analyze the relevant evidence in the text; (3) formulate an understanding of the truth that best accounts for the relevant evidence as it appears *throughout* the text.

In my analysis, I will sometimes state that Jesus spoke certain words. What I mean in every instance is that Jesus *as he is represented in the Gospel of John* spoke these words. I may sometimes omit this qualification in order to avoid the tedium of repeating it over and over, but the qualification is to be understood in every instance because we have no way of knowing exactly what Jesus said. In general, whenever I quote words from the Gospel, I do so *only* to establish that this is what the Gospel actually says, not to establish that what the Gospel says is true. To establish that the truth is true will require more than its presence in the Gospel. What is required will be addressed in Chapter 8: Believing. Fortunately for our purpose, all that really matters is that the truth is adequately represented in the Gospel - and I believe that it is.

In order to organize our quest for the truth, we will begin with what the truth is about.

What *Is* the Truth About?

The truth to which Jesus testified is about God. This much is made clear in the final words of the prologue to the Gospel of John: *No one has ever seen God. It is the only Son, who is close to the Father's heart, who has made him known.* (1:18).[8] Thus the prologue prepares us for a story about a person who made God known. Then, at the end of his public ministry, Jesus tells God in prayer, *"I have made your name known to those whom you gave me from the world."* (17:6). In biblical times, a name was understood to reveal a person's nature or character. Thus, to make God's "name" known is to make God known.[9]

The truth *is* about God, but the truth to which Jesus testified also encompasses other, related topics. The truth is also about who *we* are, expanding upon notions of *our* having been born of God that we also find in the prologue (*"But to all who received him* [Jesus], *who believed in his name, he gave power to become children of God, who were born ... of God."* 1:12-13). These same verses suggest that truth is about what we ought to be doing in light of who we are meant to be. They also inform us that in receiving Jesus (receiving the truth that he represented) we are empowered to become children of God. Becoming a child of God is one of the expressions used in the

---

[8] Here - and hereafter - I omit the extra "God" from verse 1:18
[9] See discussion in article titled, "Name," in *The Interpreters Dictionary of the Bible*, Volume 3, pp.5005-508, Abingdon Press, 1962 (15th printing, 1985).

Gospel to refer to what we might more generally think of as "salvation."

Based on what we are led to expect by the prologue, and on my reading of the Gospel as a whole, I find that the truth to which Jesus testifies therein encompasses four major topics:

- Who God Is
- Who We Are
- What We Are Meant to Be Doing, and
- Salvation

It might seem odd to anyone familiar with Christianity that I have not identified "Who Jesus Was" (or is) as one of the major topics for addressing the truth. After all, Christianity is very much concerned about who Jesus was, and Jesus does speak of himself throughout the Gospel of John. But when Jesus speaks of himself, he generally does so in order to explain the role he is playing in making the truth known, and to establish his authority for doing so (*"... I do nothing on my own, but I speak these things as the Father instructed me. And the one who sent me is with me ... "* 8:28-29). Jesus is also concerned that people recognize that he has come from, or been sent by, God (*Jesus said to them, "... I came from God and now am here. I did not come on my own, but he sent me."* 8:42). But here too he is concerned only because to recognize that he had come from God *is* to recognize the truth of what he was trying to tell us: *... the words that you* [God] *gave to me I have given them, and they have*

31

received them and know in truth that I came from you,
and they have believed that you sent me. " (17:8).

The truth to which Jesus testifies applies to him as
well as to us. And, what Jesus says about himself is often
indicative of the truth about us. Thus, while Jesus speaks
of having come from God, the Gospel makes it clear that
others have come from God as well. The prologue speaks
of those (plural) who were born of God (see 1:13), and in
the main narrative Jesus tells his listeners, *"Whoever is*
from God hears the words of God ..." (8:47). Similarly
while Jesus speaks of being "one" with the Father (*"The*
Father and I are one." 10:30), he also speaks of the
possibility of others being one with the Father: *"I ask ...*
that they may all be one. As you, Father, are in me and I
am in you, may they also be in us ... (17:20-21).

Jesus did not come to tell us about himself. He spoke
of himself in the course of testimony because what he was
saying about himself had implications for who his
listeners, and by extension we are, and could be. What
Jesus says about himself in the Gospel will come up
naturally in connection with the four major topics I have
chosen.

In the chapters that follow, we will look at what the
Gospel tells us about the author's (and indirectly Jesus')
understanding of each of the four elements of the truth. I
will then draw these elements together to form a unified
statement of the truth, and then close with some

observations about the truth and about the implications of the truth for living in this world.

In order to keep the length and complexity of chapters manageable, I have chosen to divide my four major topics into subtopics, and to devote a chapter to each subtopic. The complete sequence of chapters is:

1. Is Existence About Something?

Who God Is

2. The Nature and Existence of God

3. God's Purpose

4. How God Works

Who We Are

5. Life and Death

6. Eternal Life

7. Son of God/Son of Man

What We Are Meant to Be Doing

8. Believing

9. Loving

10. Testifying

Salvation

11. Salvation

12. The Truth Is

In the next three chapters we will look into the Gospel of John's representation of God, beginning with the nature and existence of God.

Chapter 2

THE NATURE AND EXISTENCE OF GOD

No one has ever seen God. It is the only Son[10]
who is close to the Father's heart, who has made
him known. (1:18)

In the prologue of the Gospel of John, the author
states that "no one has ever seen God" and that "the only
Son, who is close to the Father's heart, has made God
known." Then, near the end of the narrative portion of
the Gospel, Jesus reports to God, *"I have made your*
name known to those whom you gave me from the
world." (17:6). What Jesus meant in saying that he had
made God's *name* known is that he had made *God* - what
God's name stands for - known. Thus, the idea that Jesus
made God known, frames the story of Jesus' life as it is
presented in the Gospel of John.

What was it that Jesus made known about God?
What did Jesus want us to know? If we examine those
passages in the Gospel that speak of God we find
evidence relating to:
- The nature and existence of God,
- God's purpose, and

---

[10] As argued in Chapter 1 (under "Problem Passages), I have omitted
what I believe to be the spurious "God" in the NSRV translation of
verse 1:18.

- God's *modus operandi* (how God goes about achieving his purpose in this world).

In this chapter, we will examine the evidence relating to what the author of the Gospel (and thus indirectly, Jesus) wanted us to know about the nature and existence of God. God's purpose, and how God operates to achieve this purpose, will be addressed in the Chapters 3 and 4.

The Gospel employs a variety of expressions in speaking of "God." These expressions include: "the Word," "the truth," "the Father," "the Spirit" and "heaven." These different expressions refer, not to different realities, but rather to different ways of thinking and speaking about a single, transcendent reality - a reality whose locus of being lies outside the material world, a reality that accounts both for the existence of existence (that is, for there being something rather than nothing) *and* for there being a purpose behind existence.

God as the Word/the Word as God

In the opening verse of the Gospel the author redefines God as "the Word" (*In the beginning was the Word, and the Word was with God, and the Word was God. He* [or rather, it][11] *was in the beginning with God.* (1:1-2). The author introduces this new understanding

---

[11] Entries in square brackets, here and throughout this book, are not part of the NSRV translation of the Gospel. I have added them to clarify to whom or to what a word or expression refers. In this case, the pronoun refers to the Word, an "it."

of God gradually. First, the Word is said to have existed from the beginning. Next, the Word is said to have been *with* God. Finally, the author reveals what he must have had in mind all along: the Word *was* (and presumably still is) God.

Why "the Word"[12]? What would the expression, "the Word," have meant to the author of the Gospel, and to his audience, at the time in which the Gospel was being written?[13] In the broadest sense, "the word" would have been understood to be a message, perhaps a teaching (what one should know) or an instruction (what one should do). In a religious context, "the Word" would

---

[12] Or, less majestically, "the word." Ancient manuscripts were written in *either* all-upper or all-lower case letters, and so there is no warrant within the original Greek for capitalizing the Word in English. At the same time, the word is used in a special sense, and has a special meaning, in the Gospel, so the capitalization is understandable.

[13] The Gospel of John is believed by many scholars to have been completed sometime around the ninetieth year of the common era (CE, also known as AD). However, the writing of the Gospel may have begun years if not decades before it reached its final form. A claim is made in the text itself that the things written therein were written by an eyewitness to Jesus' ministry and death. The eyewitness is identified in the text only as "the disciple whom Jesus loved." This witness is said to have been present at the last supper, the crucifixion, the discovery of the empty tomb, and a posthumous appearance at the sea of Galilee. The Gospel as it has come down to us includes the work of a final editor, an editor who speaks of the original author in the third person and adds his and his colleagues' endorsement of what the eyewitness had written: *Peter turned and saw the disciple whom Jesus loved following them .... This is the disciple who is testifying to these things and has written them, and we know that his testimony is true.* 21:20-24).

have been understood as referring to a message that reveals (a) God's purpose concerning this world and (b) what is expected of us. "The Word" could also be understood to refer to the means whereby God works to bring about his purpose in this world.[14]

Why did the author of the Gospel want his readers to think of "the Word" as God? I believe that he wanted to establish the point that God cannot be thought of apart from his message. By redefining God as the Word, the author also establishes the priority of the Word over all other understandings and representations of God. The Word (the message) constitutes God's being. It is the "substance" of God.

Understanding the Word as God places constraints on God, or on who we *think of* as God. Inasmuch as the Word is God, God cannot say and do just anything. He must speak and act only in accord with the Word, the Word that has existed from the beginning. This is a good thing in that it rules out arbitrary or capricious behavior on the part of God. In Chapter 1, I pointed out that Jesus could not have agreed that the woman caught in adultery should be stoned - and still have been the person that he

---

[14] In *The Interpreter's Dictionary of the Bible, Volume 4*, p. 868. Abingdon Press, Nashville, 1962, the Word is explained as "... the characteristic means whereby God makes his will known to man in law and prophecy, and achieves his purposes in the providential guidance of the world. By it, indeed, he created the heavens and the earth."

was. Similarly, God could not have told Jesus to go along with the stoning, and still have been God.

Understanding the Word as God also has implications for how we come to know God. Inasmuch as the Word is God, we come to know God only by coming to know the Word that constitutes his being. Beyond the Word there is nothing to know, nothing that we can or need to know about God. For all practical (that is, spiritual) purposes, the Word *is* God.

The Word, the word, the words of God

Before leaving our discussion of God as the Word (or, better, the Word as God), it would be helpful to recognize and distinguish between the different ways in which "the word" is used in the Gospel of John. In English translations of the Gospel we find references to: (1) "the Word" (capitalized, singular), (2) "the word" (lower-case, singular), and (3) "the words" (lower-case, plural).

The capitalized, singular form, "the Word," appears only in the prologue of the Gospel of John, where it refers to the full message of (by and about) God, including: God's purpose, how God works to bring about his purpose in this world, and our role in connection with that purpose. It should be noted that the capitalization has been introduced into the text by the translators. The ancient Greek manuscripts of the Gospel do not mix

39

upper and lower cases in the same document. The capitalization in English translations is apparently meant to indicate that the expression is being used in a special sense, and to show respect. After all, the Word *is* God.

The lower-case, singular "the word" (or variants such as "my word," "your word," or "his word") are found throughout the main narrative in the Gospel. Sometimes "the word" refers to a specific passage from scripture: *This was to fulfill the word spoken by the prophet Isaiah. ...* (12:38) and, *It was to fulfill the word that is written in their law, 'They hated me without a cause.'* (15:25). At other times "the word" refers to specific sayings of Jesus: *"Remember the word that I said to you, 'Servants are not greater than their master ...."* (15:20) and, *This was to fulfill the word that he has spoken, "I did not lose a single one of those whom you gave me."* (18:9). But most often the lower-case, singular form is used to refer to the full message of God: *"... You have never heard his voice or seen his form, and you do not have his word abiding in you, because you do not believe in him whom he has sent."* (5:37-38) and, *"I have given them your word, and the world has hated them ..."* (17:14).

Although Jesus acknowledges that the word that he is delivering is not his own (*"... the word that you hear is not mine, but is from the Father who sent me.* (14:24), he nevertheless speaks of "my word": *"If you continue in my word, you are truly my disciples ..."* (8:31) and, *"Jesus answered him, "Those who love me will keep my word,*

40

and my Father will love them ..." (14:23). In these instances, "my word" refers to Jesus' representation, in his own words, of "the Word."

The plural form - "the words" or "my words" - refers to specific representations of the word of God, in human language. When Jesus speaks his words (plural), the listener is meant to hear the word (singular) of God: *"Whoever does not love me does not keep my words; and the word you hear is not mine, but is from the Father who sent me."* (14:24). Jesus sees his testifying to the truth *as* God working in and through him: *"The words that I say to you I do not say on my own; but the Father who dwells in me does his works."* (14:10).

God as the Truth/the Truth as God

Throughout the Gospel, Jesus is represented as speaking the word, or words, of God, - and as being aware that he is doing so. In addition to the passages cited above (verses 14:10 and 14:24), Jesus declares, *"... the one who sent me is true, and I declare to the world what I have heard from him ... I do nothing on my own, but I speak these things as the Father instructed me."* (8:26-28). And in his prayer of intercession on behalf of his disciples, Jesus reports that he has given God's words to those whom he had been given (*"I have made your name known to those whom you gave me from the world. ... for the words that you gave to me I have given to them, and they have received them ..."* 17:6-8). But

41

when brought before Pilate to explain himself, Jesus does not say that he came to speak God's *word* or *words*; instead, he states that he had been born, that he had come into the world, to testify to the *truth*.

In the prologue of the Gospel, the author refers to the Word as having been embodied by Jesus (*And the Word became flesh and lived among us* ... 1:14). Jesus does not refer to himself as "the Word" in John's Gospel. But he does refer to himself as "the truth": *Jesus said to him* [Thomas, a disciple of Jesus'], *"I am the way, and the truth, and the life."* (14:6). Jesus *was* the truth in the sense that he embodied the truth.

How are we to understand the relationship between "the truth" to which Jesus testified and "the Word" which became flesh? Clearly, the author's "Word" *is* Jesus' "truth." Further, and more direct, evidence that the Word and the truth are one-and-the-same can be found late in the Gospel, when Jesus reports to God, in his prayer of intercession on behalf of his disciples: *"I have given them your word ... Sanctify them in the truth; your word is truth."* (17:14-17). And so, inasmuch as the Word is God, we can say that *the truth* is God.

As with the Word, understanding the truth as God places constraints both on God and on our understanding of God. God cannot say just anything - and still be God; he can speak only the truth. Priority here (as it is with the Word) belongs to the truth. God does not determine what the truth is; rather, the truth determines who God is. Moreover, we can come to know God only by coming to know the truth. All we can know and all we need to know about God is the truth that constitutes his being.[15] Thus, it is not surprising that Jesus thought of himself as having come to testify to the truth. In doing so, he was making God known.

God as the Father/the Father as God

Jesus does not explicitly refer to God as either "the Word" or "the truth" in the Gospel of John. He refers to God simply as "God," or as "the Father," or indirectly, as "him who sent me." Although Jesus sometimes speaks of God as "*my* Father," he is not thinking of God as his father in an exclusive sense. He understands that God could be our Father as well as his own. This is made clear when, after his death, Jesus appears to Mary Magdalene and advises her, *"Do not hold on to me, because I have not yet ascended to the Father. But go to my brothers and say to them, "I am ascending to my*

---

[15] The twin ideas - that the truth is God and that priority belongs to the truth - have been rediscovered in modern times. Several years ago, by chance, I came across a refrigerator magnet which reads, "THERE IS NO HIGHER GOD THAN TRUTH," and attributes this saying to Mahatma Gandhi (Ephemera Inc. 1998, stock #9331). More recently, and also by chance, I found myself watching a movie (*Water*, 2005) in which Gandhi is represented as telling a crowd at a railway station, "Live long. Be happy. My dear brothers and sisters, for a long time I believed that God is truth. But today I know that truth is God. The pursuit of truth is invaluable for me. I trust it will be the same for you."

Father and your Father, to my God and your God."
(20:17). God is the father of all those whom Jesus
considers to be his brothers (and, no doubt, his sisters).

What does Jesus mean when he refers to God as his,
and his brothers', Father? Although Jesus says that he
owes his life to the Father (*"Just as the living Father
sent me, and I live because of the Father ..."* 6:57), he is
not thinking of God as anyone's father in the material
sense. Rather, Jesus is thinking of God as his, and
perhaps our, father in a spiritual or transcendent sense.
As will be made clear in Chapter 6, the "life" referred to
by the author in the prologue (*What has come into being
in it* [in the Word] *was life, and life was the light of all
people.* 1:3-4) and alluded to by Jesus in verse 6:57 is
"eternal life," a transcendent state of being in relation to
God. God can thus be thought of as the father of a
person's transcendent (or spiritual) self. As the author of
the Gospel put it, those who received Jesus (his message)
and believed in his name (as he taught) were those who
were *born, not of blood* or *of the will of the flesh or of
the will of man, but of God.* (1:12-13).

God can also be thought of as one's Father in a more
conventional sense. Throughout the Gospel, God plays
the role of a conventional, albeit ideal, father:

  - The Father loves the Son (*The Father loves the Son
    and has placed all things in his hands.* 3:35),

- The Father serves as a role model (*But Jesus answered them, "My Father is still working, and I also am working. ... Very truly I tell you, the Son can do nothing on his own, but only what he sees the Father doing; for whatever the Father does, the Son does likewise."* 5:17-19),

- The Father gives the son work to do (*"... The works that the Father has given me to complete, the very works that I am doing, testify on my behalf that the Father has sent me."* (5:36),

- The Father provides instruction (*"... I do nothing on my own, but I speak these things as the Father instructed me."* (8:28), and

- The Father inspires the Son (*"He whom God has sent speaks the words of God, for he gives the Spirit without measure."* 3:34).

God is a person's Father, however, only inasmuch as that person brings his or her intention and behavior into accord with the truth. In the Gospel, this notion is represented in an argument that Jesus has with some listeners who once did, but no longer do, believe in him. The argument begins when Jesus tells his listeners, *"If you continue in my word, you are truly my disciples; and you will know the truth, and the truth will make you free."* (8:31). Jesus' listeners reply that they are descendants of Abraham and have never been slaves to anyone. They then ask Jesus what he means by saying they will be made free.

The Nature and Existence of God

In his answer, Jesus suggests that his listeners are slaves to sin (*"Very truly, I tell you, everyone who commits sin is a slave to sin. The slave does not have a permanent place in the household; the son has a place there forever. So, if the Son makes you free, you will be free indeed."* 8:34-36). Jesus acknowledges that, although his listeners are descendants of Abraham in the material sense, their behavior reveals their spiritual separation from the word, and thus also from Abraham:

> *"I know that you are descendants of Abraham; yet you look for an opportunity to kill me, because there is no place in you for my word. ... If you were Abraham's children, you would be doing what Abraham did, but now <u>you are trying to kill me, a man who has told you the truth that I heard from God</u>. This is not what Abraham did."* (8:37-40).

When his listeners insist that God *is* their father, Jesus replies,

> "<u>If God were your Father, you would love me</u>, for I came from God ... Why do you not understand what I say? It is because <u>you cannot accept my word. You are from your father the devil, and you choose to do your father's desires. He was a murderer from the beginning and does not stand in the truth</u>, because there is no truth in him. When he lies, he speaks according to his own nature, for he is a liar and the father of lies." (8:42-44).

From Jesus' point-of-view, one's true (spiritual) paternity is revealed not by one's genealogy but rather by one's behavior. By telling his opponents that their father is the father of lies, Jesus is also suggesting that they are participating in these lies, in their misrepresentations of the truth, and thus of God.

What is the lie to which Jesus' opponents testify? The lie is that God can be served by violence, by persecution and murder. Much later in the Gospel, in preparing his followers for his death and departure, Jesus warns his them of a persecution to come: *"They will put you out of the synagogues. Indeed, an hour is coming when those who kill you will think that by doing so they are offering worship to God"* (16:2). This is the lie that has been told again and again, from the beginning. Not much has changed in this respect over the years. People have been, and continue to be put out of houses of worship, persecuted and murdered in the name of "God."

Jesus' representation of God as the Father is fully compatible with the author's representation of God as the Word. While the author tells us that the Word brings life ("... *What has come into being in [it] was life* ...verses 1:3-4), Jesus tells us that the Father brings life (*"Indeed, just as the Father raises the dead and gives them life, so also the Son gives life ...."* 5:21).

God as Spirit

In the Gospel of John, the activity of God in this world is sometimes attributed to "the Spirit." We are first introduced to the Spirit in John the Baptist's testimony to Jesus:

> *The next day he* [John the Baptist] *saw Jesus coming toward him and declared, "Here is the lamb of God who takes away the sin of the world! ... I saw the Spirit descending from heaven like a dove, and it remained on him. I myself did not know him, but the one who sent me to baptize with water said to me, 'He on whom you see the Spirit descend and remain is the one who baptizes with the Holy Spirit.' And I myself have seen and have testified that this is the Son of God."* (1:29-34).

In this passage, John testifies that he "saw the Spirit descending from heaven like a dove ..." But did the Baptist see the Spirit in the literal, that is the material, sense? Who can rule it out? But what is more likely is that, in this passage, the Baptist (or the author of the Gospel) was employing figurative language to make the point that the Baptist somehow recognized Jesus as the "lamb of God"[16] and "Son of God." Something told him who Jesus was, and the Baptist recognized that something as the Spirit. I say that the figurative intention

---

[16] The "lamb of God" here is an allusion to Isaiah 53:7 in which the author refers to a personified Israel as the "servant" of God who "like a lamb" was led to the slaughter.

is more likely because the Baptist didn't say he saw an actual dove; rather he said he saw the spirit descending *like a dove.* While a literal sighting of the spirit is unlikely, a figurative sighting is highly likely. Figurative (that is, non-literal) language is used throughout the Gospel of John. Toward the end of his ministry, Jesus explains to his disciples, *"I have said these things to you in figures of speech. The hour is coming when I will no longer speak to you in figures, but will tell you plainly of the Father."* (16:25).

Jesus' first mentions the Spirit in his conversation with Nicodemus, in verses 3:1-10 of the Gospel. In this conversation, Jesus tells Nicodemus, *"... no one can see the kingdom of God without being born from above."*[17] (3:3). And when Nicodemus does not understand, Jesus explains,

> *"... no one can enter the kingdom of God without being <u>born of water and Spirit</u>.*[18] *What is born of the flesh is flesh, and what is <u>born of the Spirit</u> is*

---

[17] Some English translations (e.g., the King James Version and the New International Version) read "born again" rather than "born from above" in verse 3:7). While either translation could make sense if the verse is viewed in isolation, "born from above" is the only reading that is consistent with the larger context in which it is embedded, i.e., with the Gospel of John as a whole. This issue is addressed more thoroughly in Chapter 6.

[18] The words, "water and," in verse 3:5 seem out of place. They do not appear before "spirit" in the other verses in the same passage. Moreover, "water and" is redundant inasmuch as the Spirit is represented figuratively *as* water in the Gospel of John.

*spirit. Do not be astonished that I said to you,
'You must be born from above.' The wind blows
where it chooses, and you hear the sound of it, ...
So it is with everyone who is <u>born of the Spirit</u>.*"
(3:5-8).

In these verses, the action of the Spirit accounts for one's
ability to enter the kingdom of God: no one can enter
without being "born of water and Spirit." It also
accounts for one entering into spiritual existence, a
transcendent state of being: "what is born of the Spirit is
spirit." The Spirit itself decides upon whom it will
descend. In the words of the Gospel, it "blows where it
chooses." We recognize the work ("hear the sound") of
the Spirit, but otherwise we cannot explain its working
(we "do not know where it comes from or where it
goes").

Note that the role assigned to the Spirit in verses 3:3-
8 is essentially the role attributed to God in the prologue
(*But to all who received him, who believed in his name,
he gave power to become children of God, who were
born, not ... of the flesh ... but of God* (1:12-13). In
Jesus' conversation with Nicodemus, one must be born
of the spirit (or, equivalently, from above) to enter the
kingdom of God. In the prologue, one must be born of
God to be enabled to become a child of God. In both
passages, being born of the transcendent (God or the
Spirit) is contrasted with being born of the flesh.

The Spirit gives life: *"It is the spirit that gives life; the flesh is useless. The words that I have spoken to you are spirit and life."* (6:63). The words of Jesus (from God) are "spirit and life." To hear and to recognize the truth to which Jesus testified is to be informed by the Spirit. And to recognize the truth and take it to heart is to have life, eternal life. Again, in verse 6:63, the spirit plays the role attributed to the Word in the prologue. Here life is said to be given by the spirit; in the prologue, life is said to come into being through the Word (*What has come into being in it* [the Word] *was life ...* 1:3-4a).

In the Gospel of John, the Spirit is referred to variously as: the Holy Spirit, the Spirit, and the Spirit of truth. Anticipating his own death, Jesus attempts to reassure his disciples by telling them that after he is gone the Father will send them another "advocate," an advocate he then identifies as "the Spirit of truth":

> *"If you love me, you will keep my commandments. And I will ask the Father, and he will give you another Advocate, to be with you forever. This is the Spirit of truth, whom the world cannot receive, because it neither sees him nor knows him. You know him, because he abides with you, and he will be in you."* (14:15-17).

This passage reveals that Jesus saw himself as an advocate, the "other" advocate being the "Spirit of truth." That Jesus saw himself as an advocate for the truth is consistent with his understanding that he had been born, that he had come into the world, to testify to the truth.

Jesus also directly refers to God as spirit in John's Gospel:

> *"But the hour is now coming, and is now here, when the true worshipers will worship the Father in spirit and truth, for the Father seeks such as these to worship him. <u>God is spirit, and those who worship him must worship in spirit and truth.</u>"* (4:23-24).

God as Place

The transcendent reality behind existence is also represented in the Gospel of John as the *place* wherein God resides, and from which he operates. Just as it is sometimes convenient to speak of a source of the Word (i.e., God), it is sometimes convenient, to refer to the location of this source. That location - what we might think of as the "locus-of-being" of God - is referred to in the Gospel of John as "heaven," or as being "up, or "above."

Heaven is first mentioned in the Gospel of John when Jesus assures Nathanael, who has just recognized him as the Son of God, *"Very truly, I tell you, <u>you will see heaven opened and the angels of God ascending and descending upon the Son of Man.</u>"* (1:51). The Greek word translated as "angel" means messenger. And so, in this verse, Jesus is telling Nathanael that he will come to see messengers of God passing back and forth between, the Son of Man[19] and God.

Jesus understood that in testifying to the truth, he would be speaking of "heavenly" things. This can be seen when he asks Nicodemus, *"If I have told you about earthly things and you do not believe, how can you believe if I tell you of heavenly things?"* (3:12). Jesus also speaks of heavenly things in connection with the true "bread from heaven":

> *Then Jesus said to them, "Very truly, I tell you, it was not Moses who gave you the bread from heaven, but it is my Father who gives you the true bread from heaven. For the bread of God is that which comes down from heaven and gives life to the world."* (6:32-33).

The true bread in this passage, "that which ... gives life to the world," is of course the Word, the word of God, the truth to which Jesus was testifying.

---

[19] During the time in which Jesus taught, and the Gospel was being written, the expression, "the son of man" was understood, in general usage, to mean simply a human being. However, the expression, "the Son of Man," has a special meaning in John's Gospel, a meaning that will be addressed in Chapter 7 (Son of Man/Son of God).

Heaven is the place from which the Word emanates. Heaven is also the place from which a person can be said to have descended and ascended. As Jesus explains to Nicodemus, *"No one has ascended into heaven except the one who descended from heaven, the Son of Man."* (3:13). Who is this "Son of Man' who had descended from Heaven? Surely, Jesus refers to himself when he refers to "the one who has descended," for he later tells a crowd that has followed him, *" ... I have come down from heaven, not to do my own will, but the will of him who sent me."* (6:38). Jesus' identity as the Son of Man is made explicit later when he tells some opponents that when he is "lifted up" (raised up on the cross at his execution), even they will see that he is the Son of Man: *So Jesus said, "When you have lifted up the Son of Man, then you will realize that I am he ... "* (8:28).

It is clear that Jesus is referring to himself when he speaks of the Son of Man. However, he may be referring to others as well - that is, he may be using the term in a corporate sense. We will address to whom the expression, "the Son of Man" refers in more detail in Chapter 7 (Son of Man/Son of God). For the present, suffice it to say that "heaven" is the name given to the locus-of-being of God. Heaven is it's name, but where is heaven?

Heaven is referred to in John's Gospel as being "up," and "above." After his farewell speech to his disciples, Jesus looks up and tells the Father that the time for his

The Nature and Existence of God

death has come: *After Jesus had spoken these words, he looked up to heaven and said, "Father, the hour has come to glorify your Son ..."* (17:1). That heaven is "up" is not surprising inasmuch as the Greek word translated here as "heaven" can also mean "sky." Heaven is also spoken of directionally as "above" in the Gospel. Thus in verse 3:31 we find: *The one who comes from above is above all ... The one who comes from heaven is above all.*

Being "from above" is just another way of saying, being "from heaven." And, not surprisingly, the bread (the word of God) is said to come "down" from heaven: *... the bread of God is that which comes down from heaven and gives life to the world.* (6:32). Already we see that a person can come down from heaven, and the word of God (the Word, or truth) can come down from heaven. It may be premature to suggest this, but perhaps when the Word comes down from heaven it brings a person's true self with it. Or, we might say, when the truth dawns on us, our true self comes into being.

Is heaven really "up" or "above" in the literal sense? No. To say that heaven is up or above is a figurative way of saying that God's or, equivalently, the truth's locus of being and base of operations lie outside the material world.

Although God is transcendent, he is nevertheless present and at work in this world. While God cannot be

seen (*"No one has ever seen God. ...."* 1:18),
manifestations of his influence can be "seen" (perceived
and recognized as such). The operation of the
transcendent in this world can be seen in people's
attraction to, and recognition of, the truth; and their
deciding to bring their life into accord with the truth.
And personally, *we* experience the influence of the
transcendent in our own life in our being drawn to the
truth, in our recognizing the truth, and in our sense of
responsibility to act on the truth. Recognizing and acting
in accord with the truth will be addressed in Part III
(What We Are Meant To Be Doing, Chapters 8-10).

The Priority of the Truth

If we are to recognize a hierarchy among the various
representations of God (God, the Word, the truth, the
Father, the Spirit, heaven/above), I suggest that we
assign the highest place to the truth. The truth
constitutes the substance of each of the other
representations of the transcendent. Our understanding
of each representation is helpful only inasmuch as it
reflects the truth. Visually we might think of the truth as
the light shining from above, giving substance to: God,
the Word, the Father, the Spirit, heaven - and, as I will
argue in Chapter 7, the Son of Man.

Metaphysics and the Gospel

The prologue to the Gospel of John introduces a metaphysical framework for understanding Jesus' life, and the truth to which he testified. Metaphysics has been defined as "the branch of philosophy that treats of first principles, includes ontology and cosmology, and is intimately connected with epistemology."[20] Although the term "metaphysics" does not appear in the Gospel of John, the Gospel is very much concerned with the first principles behind being, and with epistemology (with the nature of existence and knowledge). The Gospel begins by revealing an unseen reality "behind" material existence - the Word/God. This transcendent reality is then invoked by the author in order to account both for existence (all things) having come into being *and* for there being a purpose behind existence.

Is metaphysics, the use of metaphysical language, really necessary? Must one invoke notions like the Word, God, the Father, and the Spirit in order to speak of the truth? Yes. Notions such as the purpose behind, and the truth about, existence are not material facts. Nothing within existence - no observable facts or combination of facts and logical reasoning - can account for there being, or *not* being, a purpose behind existence. Nothing within existence can account for existence being *either* about

---

[20] *Random House Webster's College Dictionary*, Random House, New York, 1999.

something *or* about nothing. To argue either position we will need to refer to a source of purpose and meaning (or of purposelessness and meaninglessness) that lies outside material existence. In short, we need to employ metaphysical language.

We could mask our dependence on a metaphysical source of purpose and meaning. For example, in reference to the story of the woman caught in adultery (verses 8:2-11, see discussion in Chapter 1), we could say that "something" told Jesus that stoning the woman caught in adultery would be wrong - even though it was called for in scripture. To say that "something" told Jesus what to say to the scribes and Pharisees, would avoid having to say that God (or the Word, or truth) told him what to say. But that something *is* the transcendent, *is* the functional equivalent of God. So we might as well take advantage of the metaphysics of the Fourth Gospel as a language of convenience.

The metaphysical language of the Fourth Gospel is convenient in several respects. It is a convenient way of accounting for existence and for there being a purpose behind existence, and hence for there being such a thing as truth, as *the* truth. It is also a convenient way of explaining how God operates in this world, and how it is that the truth becomes known and appropriated. While metaphysical language is convenient, it is important to recognize that the metaphysics doesn't determine the truth. It is the truth that should determine the content of our metaphysics.

Does God Exist?

Inasmuch as the Word is God, the question, "does God exist?" becomes, does the Word (or, equivalently, the truth) exist? The author of the Gospel of John is telling us that it does. He does this by assigning to the Word/truth the role of creator: *All things came into being through it* [the Word]*, and without it nothing came into being ...* (1:3). In this verse, the Word is said to have brought existence ("all things") into being. Moreover, inasmuch as the Word pre-existed everything else (*In the beginning was the Word ...* 1:1), and the Word encompasses a purpose, the Gospel is telling us that there *is* a purpose behind existence, and that this purpose was not an afterthought. This is just what one would expect of a purpose behind existence.

In the prologue, the author of the Gospel of John is saying that there is a purpose behind existence. And as we read through the main narrative we find Jesus saying that there is too. But whether the author of the Gospel, or Jesus as represented in the Gospel, says that there is a purpose behind existence does not make it so. And of course whether *we* say there is a purpose, or that there isn't, doesn't make it so either. The purpose was either there from the beginning or not at all.

Since it is not possible to establish the truth scientifically; how can we know whether there is a purpose or not? Rather than attempt to deal with the existence of God - or of a purpose behind existence - in the abstract, I propose that we listen to what the Gospel says the purpose is, and then ask ourselves if what the Gospel (and Jesus as represented in the Gospel) is saying strikes us as true. If it does, then we have our own answer. Toward that end (coming up with our own answer), the next chapter will address the Gospel's representation of God's purpose, the purpose behind existence.

The *purpose* behind existence is just one element of the larger truth behind existence. The truth also encompasses: how God (the Word, the truth) operates to realize his (its) purpose, who we are (including who we are meant to be), what we are meant to be doing, and salvation. Accordingly, I suggest that we wait until the entire truth is before us before deciding what our relationship to the truth is.

Points to Keep in Mind

- **The Word/truth *is* God. The truth constitutes God's being; it makes him who he is. We can think of the truth as the "substance" of God.**

- **God is not free to say or do just anything; he can speak and act only in accord with the** truth. Thus, God is not capricious or arbitrary.

- We come to know God by, and only by coming to know the truth that constitutes his being.

- God (the Word, the truth) is transcendent; its locus of being lies outside the material world.

- Inasmuch as there *is* a truth behind existence, inasmuch as the truth exists, God exists.

Chapter 3

GOD'S PURPOSE

"For God so loved the world that he gave his only Son, so that everyone who believes in him may not perish but may have eternal life. (3:16)

The author's (and Jesus') understanding of God's purpose (the purpose behind existence) is revealed in those passages in the Gospel of John that speak of: (a) What God does, (b) God's purposes in sending his Son into the world, (c) God's will and motivation, and (d) Jesus' "new commandment" to his disciples. We will now look at these passages, identify the various purposes revealed in them, and, then - taking into account the relationships among these purposes - identify God's ultimate purpose, *the* purpose behind existence.

What God Does

One of God's purposes is suggested early in the prologue to the Gospel of John, after the author tells us that the Word - the Word which is God - brought "all things" into being: *All things came into being through it [the Word] and without it not one thing came into being.* (1:3a). The author then directs our attention to one thing in particular - "life": *What has come into being in it [the Word] was life* ... (1:3b-4a). The Word is said to have brought life into being, but the life with which God, and

63

the Gospel, is most concerned is not life in the biological sense, but rather "eternal life," a transcendent state of being, a state of being in relation to God. What eternal life is will be examined in detail, in Chapters 5 (Life and Death) and 6 (Eternal Life). In this chapter our focus will be on God's purpose.

God's Purposes in Sending His Son

Two statements of God's purpose in sending his Son into the world appear at the end of Jesus' conversation with a Pharisee[21] named Nicodemus. In this conversation Jesus tells Nicodemus (and/or the author tells the reader[22]),

> *"For God so loved the world that he gave his only Son, so that everyone who believes in him may not perish but may have eternal life."* (3:16), and

---

[21] "The name of a party or sect within Judaism, mentioned frequently in the Gospels. They centered their religious outlook on the observance of the law and so may be regarded as in the heritage of Ezra rather than that of the prophets. It was apparently on this account that Jesus and they came into such conflict." *Dictionary of Religion and Philosophy* by Geddes MacGregor, Paragon House, New York, 1989.

[22] The NRSV translation places quotation marks around verses 3:16-21, suggesting that they are the continuation of Jesus' conversation with Nicodemus. However, in a footnote, the NRSV notes that some interpreters maintain that the words of Jesus' end just before verse 3:16.

"Indeed, God did not send the Son into the world to condemn the world, but in order that the world might be saved through him." (3:17).

These two verses present us with two different representations of God's purpose. The first verse suggests that God's purpose is that believers may be brought to have eternal life. The second verse suggests that God's purpose is to save the world.

God's Will

During his "discourse on the bread of life " (verses 6:25-40), Jesus explains his purpose in having come down from heaven, and in the process speaks of God's "will":

... I have come down from heaven not to do my own will, but the will of him who sent me. And this is the will of him who sent me, that I should lose [none]²³ of all [who] he has given me, but raise [them] up on the last day. (6:38-39), and

This is indeed the will of my Father, that all who see the Son and believe in him may have eternal

---

²³ My translation here diverges from the NRSV translation. The words in square brackets represent the changes I have made. The resulting text is well within the possible range of meanings of the original Greek, and better fits both the immediate and larger contexts of the passage. The changes also agree with the translation found in the New International Version (NIV) of this Gospel.]

life; and I will raise them up on the last day.
(6:40).

Here we have two, side-by-side statements of God's will.
In the first (verses 6:38-39) God's will is said to be that
Jesus should not lose any of those who have been given to
him, but rather he should "raise them up on the last day."
In the second (verse 6:40) God's will is said to be "that all
who see the Son and believe in him may have eternal
life," and "be raised up on the last day." These two
statements represent two ways of saying essentially the
same thing. Accordingly, to not be lost (6:38-39) is to
have eternal life (6:40). And to have been "given" by
God to Jesus (6:38-39) is to "see the Son and believe in
him." (6:40) Both passages conclude by saying that
Jesus is to raise up those who see and believe in him (or,
equivalently, those have been given to him) on the last
day. Together, the two passages reinforce the idea,
already expressed in verses 3:16-17, that God's purpose in
sending Jesus was that people who believe in "the Son"
may have eternal life.

God's Motivation

Verse 3:16 tells us that God "so loved the world" that
he sent his only Son so that everyone who believed in him
might have eternal life. God was motivated by love.
That God loved (and presumably still loves) the world is
also expressed in other passages in the Gospel. Late in
his public ministry, Jesus tells his disciples that they need

only ask God for anything in his (Jesus') name and God will grant it: *"On that day you will ask nothing of me. Very truly, I tell you, if you ask anything of the Father in my name, he will give it to you"* (16:23). Then, only a few verses later, Jesus tells the disciples that the day is coming when they will ask things of God directly:

> *"On that day you will ask in my name. I do not say to you that I will ask the Father on your behalf; for the Father himself loves you, because you have loved me and have believed that I came from God."* (16:26-27).

God's love for the disciples is not unlike his love for Jesus. This point is made when, during his prayer of intercession on behalf of his disciples, Jesus tells the Father,

> *"The glory that you have given me I have given them ... so that the world may know that you have sent me and have loved them even as you have loved me."* (17:22-23).

Verses 16:26-27 might be understood to say that God loves the disciples *because* they have loved Jesus and have believed that he came from God. In other words, the passage might be understood to be saying that God's love for the disciples was conditional, conditioned on their love for Jesus. But there is another possibility. The author might have meant that the disciple's love of Jesus,

and their belief that he had come from God, is *evidence of*
God's love. In other words, verse 16:27 could be
understood to be saying: "the Father himself loves you,
and we know this because you have loved me and have
believed that I came from God." In this sense, one's
recognition that Jesus had come from God is itself a gift
from God. This reading of verses 16:26-27 supports an
understanding that God's love is unconditional. That
God's love *is* unconditional is also implicit in verse 3:16,
wherein God's love for the world is represented as having
existing *prior to* the sending of the Son into the world,
and before anyone's response to Jesus.

God loves the world, he loves the disciples, and he
also loves the Son: *The Father loves the Son and has
placed all things in his hands* (3:35) and, in Jesus' words,
*"The Father loves the son and shows him all that he
himself is doing ..."* (5:20). Later Jesus explains, *"For this
reason the Father loves me, because I lay down my life in
order to take it up again."* (10:17). Here again, it might
seem that God's love is conditional, conditioned on Jesus
laying down his life. But this would be a
misunderstanding. God's love pre-existed anything that
Jesus did. As Jesus tells the Father just prior to his arrest,
"... you loved me before the foundation of the world."
(17:24).

God's Motivation *as* His Purpose

God's motivation, his love for the world, can also be thought of as his purpose. Evidence to support this understanding can be found in connection with Jesus' purpose in having come into the world. Jesus' purpose in having come into the world - as he understood it - was to testify to the truth: *"For this I was born, and for this I came into the world, to testify to the truth."* (18:37). The author of the Gospel tells us that, in his testimony, Jesus made God known: *It is the only Son, who is close to the Father's heart, who has made him known.* (1:18). And in the main narrative, Jesus reveals that his purpose in making God known was so that God's love would be in those who would come to believe: *"I made your name known to them, and I will make it known, <u>so that the love with which you have loved me may be in them</u>, and I in them."* (17:26). Thus, Jesus testified so that those who would come to know the truth would come to embody divine love.

That bringing divine love into being in this world can be thought of as God's purpose is consistent with the "new commandment" that Jesus gives to his disciples: *"<u>I give you a new commandment, that you love one another</u>. Just as I have loved you, you also should love one another."* (13:34) and by Jesus' criterion for true discipleship: *"By this everyone will know that you are my disciples, if you have love for one another."* (13:35).

69

The Purpose behind Existence

God's purpose is represented in the Gospel of John variously as being: (1) to bring people to eternal life, (2) to save the world, and (3) to bring divine love into being in this world. How are we to understand the relationships among these three representations of God's purpose?

First, as will be established in later chapters, these three purposes are mutually consistent and supportive. Those who believe, and bring their lives into accord with, the truth have eternal life. They recognize their personal responsibility to love others and to testify to the truth. And by believing, loving and testifying to the truth they are saved from meaninglessness and the finality of natural death. At the same time, a hierarchy of purposes does exist in the Gospel, a hierarchy in which the bringing of divine love (selfless and unconditional love) into being is God's ultimate purpose.

In the Gospel of John, love is the beginning and the end of everything that God does. It is God's motivation in sending Jesus into the world. And love is the end toward which the truth leads. Jesus testifies to the truth, and those who believe the truth recognize their responsibility to love others and to testify to the truth themselves - so that others might come to believe and love. To love one another is the only commandment that Jesus gives to his disciples. Finally, loving one another is the single criterion by which it is revealed that one is a true follower of Jesus. In short, love is the *sine qua non* of discipleship; without love nothing matters, nothing will have mattered.

To bring love into being, to infuse this otherwise merely material and thus meaningless world with love, is the purpose behind existence. Eternal life and salvation are natural (actually, supernatural) consequences of loving others. Eternal life and salvation come to those who adopt God's purpose as their own and participate in the bringing of love into being.

That there *is* a purpose behind existence, and that this purpose is to bring love into being, are elements of the truth behind existence. The truth to which Jesus testified also encompasses *how* God works to realize his purpose. How he works will be taken up next, in Chapter 4.

Points to Keep in Mind

- **God's ultimate purpose - the purpose behind existence - is to bring love into being, to infuse this otherwise merely material, and thus meaningless, world with divine (selfless and unconditional) love.**

- **Eternal life and salvation are natural (or rather, supernatural) consequences of one's love for others.**

Chapter 4

HOW GOD WORKS

He whom God has sent speaks the words of God,
for he gives the Spirit without measure. The
Father loves the Son and has placed all things in
his hands. (3:34-35)

God works to realize his purpose - or we could say
that the truth works to realize its purpose - through people
in this world. God reveals the truth directly to
individuals, sends them to testify to the truth, draws
people to the truth, and participates in their coming to
know - and to bring their lives into accord with - the truth.
In so doing, God invites and enables us to participate in
realizing the purpose behind existence, to be his agents in
the task of bringing of love into being. In this chapter we
will look at what the Gospel of John tells us about each of
these aspects of his mode of operating in this world.

God Reveals the Truth to Individuals

In the Gospel of John, God is represented as having
revealed the truth directly to: John the Baptist, Jesus,
unnamed colleagues of Jesus, the Son, "the one who
comes from above," and Jesus' disciples.

To John the Baptist

In the Gospel, God is represented as having spoken
directly to John the Baptist. In the prologue to the
Gospel, the author tells us that the Baptist had been sent
by God to testify to the light: *There was a man sent from
God, whose name was John. He came as a witness to
testify to the light, so that all might believe through him*
(1:6-7). "The light" in this verse is generally taken to be a
reference to Jesus - but it could as well refer to the Word
(or the truth) to which Jesus would testify. In fact, later in
the Gospel, Jesus tells his listeners that the Baptist had
testified to the truth (*"You sent messengers to John, and
he testified to the truth."* 5:33). In any case, the Baptist is
said to have testified to the light (Jesus) so that all might
come to believe through him. During his testimony, the
Baptist explains how he was able to recognize Jesus for
who he was:

> *And John Testified, "I saw the Spirit descending
> from heaven like a dove, and it remained on him.
> I myself did not know him, but the one who sent
> me to baptize with water* [God] *said to me, 'He on
> whom you see the Spirit descend and remain is the
> one who baptizes with the Holy Spirit.' And I
> myself have seen and have testified that this is the
> Son of God."* (1:32-33).

In this passage, God is represented as having spoken
specific words to John. But is what the Baptist says in

this passage *the* truth? No. The truth to which Jesus testifies in the Gospel is a much larger truth, a truth which encompasses more than Jesus' identity and his relationship to God. The Baptist's testimony here is merely meant to prepare his listeners, and readers of John's Gospel, to take Jesus and his testimony seriously.

To Jesus

God is also represented as having spoken directly to Jesus. On the day following the Festival of Booths[24], Jesus attempts to explain himself to a puzzled, and somewhat hostile, audience. Finally, in exasperation, Jesus exclaims,

> *"Why do I speak to you at all? I have much to say about you, and much to condemn; but the one who sent me is true, and I declare to the world what I have heard from him"* (8:25-26).

Realizing that his listeners still do not accept what he is saying, Jesus continues,

---

[24] The Festival (or Feast) of Booths is "one of the three biblically mandated festivals Shalosh regalim on which Hebrews were commanded to make a pilgrimage to the Temple in Jerusalem" (Wikipedia, 4/13/12), "One of Israel's three great annual festivals, celebrated with great joy in autumn, at the completion of the the agricultural year, to recall Israel's wilderness pilgrimage and, apparently, as a renewal of the covenant; commonly known as Tabernacles", *The Interpreter's Dictionary of the Bible*, Volume I (A-D), p. 455-458, Abbington Press, Nashville, 1962.

"... I do nothing on my own, but I speak these things <u>as the Father instructed me</u>. And the one who sent me is with me; he has not left me alone ..." (8:28-29).

In both of these passages, Jesus claims that he has been speaking what he had heard directly from God. Similar claims are made in later passages, for example:

"... I have not spoken on my own, <u>but the Father who sent me has himself given me a commandment about what to say and what to speak</u>. ... What I speak, therefore, I speak just <u>as the Father has told me</u>." (12:49-50),

"Do you not believe that I am in the Father and the Father is in me? <u>The words that I say to you I do not speak on my own;</u> but the Father who dwells in me does his works." (14:10), and

"... <u>the words that you</u> [the Father] <u>gave to me</u> I have given to them [the disciples]; and they have received them and know in truth that I came from you ..." (17:8).

In saying that "the one who sent me is with me; he has not left me alone" (8:29), Jesus implies that he was in continuous communication with the Father during his public ministry. This is understandable in light of the even stronger claim he makes in verse 14:10 (*"I am in the*

Father and the Father is in me ... the Father who dwells in me does his works.").

God not only *spoke* the truth to Jesus but also *showed* Jesus what he himself was doing: *"I declare what I have seen in the Father's presence; as for you, you should do what you have heard from the Father."* (8:38). In this verse, Jesus switches from "have seen" to "have heard." This is a distinction without a real difference inasmuch as seeing and hearing are alternative ways of receiving the truth directly from God." In this case, Jesus does not actually expect his listeners to do what they have heard from *the* Father (God). Rather, he expects that they will do what *their* father does, and that's not good:

> *"You are indeed doing what your father does."* ...
> *"You are from your father the devil, and you choose to do your father's desires. He was a murderer from the beginning and does not stand in the truth, because there is no truth in him..."*
> (8:41-44).

As Jesus saw it, a person's behavior reveals who the person's true father is.

To unnamed colleagues of Jesus

God is represented as having communicated directly with unnamed colleagues of Jesus. At the end of his conversation with Nicodemus, Jesus declares, *"Very* *truly, I tell you, <u>we</u> speak of what <u>we</u> know and testify to what <u>we</u> have seen; yet you do not receive <u>our</u> testimony."* (3:11). The "we" and "our" in this verse indicates that Jesus saw himself as working alongside colleagues who, like him, had seen the truth.

To the Son

God is represented as having communicated directly with "the Son of Man." That God would do so is first suggested in the Gospel when Jesus tells an early follower, Nathanael, *"Very truly, I tell you, <u>you will see heaven opened and the angels of God ascending and descending on the Son of Man.</u>"* (1:51). The Greek word translated here as "angels" means "messengers." In this verse, Jesus is telling Nathanael that he will see messengers of God going back and forth between God and "the Son of Man." That God reveals, and will continue to reveal, the truth directly to the Son is made even more explicit in this passage:

> *Jesus said to them, "Very truly, I tell you, <u>the Son can do nothing on his own, but only what he sees the Father doing</u>; for whatever the Father does, the Son does likewise. <u>The Father loves the Son and shows him all that he himself is doing</u>; and he will show him greater works than these, so that you will be astonished."* (5:19-20).

The expression, "the Son," in both of these passages certainly applies to Jesus. But, as I will argue in Chapter 7 (Son of Man/Son of God), it also applies to *any*one who has come to believe, and has brought his or her life into accord with, the truth.

To the one who comes from above/heaven/God

God also reveals the truth directly to "the one who comes from above (or, equivalently, from heaven or from God)":

> *"The one who comes from above is above all; the one who is of the earth belongs to the earth and speaks of earthly things. The one who comes from heaven is above all. He testifies to what he has seen and heard* .... (3:31-32).

The one who comes from heaven has both "seen and heard" the truth from God. But who is "the one who comes from above"? The expression certainly applies to Jesus. He has come from above, and he testifies to what he has seen and heard. Nevertheless, the statement does not explicitly identify "the one" as Jesus. The definite article in "the one who comes from above" need not be interpreted as referring to a particular person. In the Greek, the definite article appears by itself (without a following noun) and refers to "one," that is, to anyone who comes from above (or from heaven). The same grammatical construction (the definite article without a noun) is used in the same sentence to refer "the one who is of the earth," and this "one" undoubtedly refers to anyone who belongs to the earth.

Later in the Gospel Jesus also tells some opponents that whoever is from God hears the words of God - and that anyone who has *not* come from God does *not* hear the words of God: *"Whoever is from God hears the words of God. The reason you do not hear them* [the words of God] *is that you are not from God."* (8:47). "Whoever" in this verse clearly refers to a category of people. And Jesus is saying here that anyone who is able to hear the words of God must be from God.

To Jesus' disciples

The Gospel tells us that God will also speak to Jesus' disciples. In anticipation of his execution, Jesus reassures his disciples that God will send them "another Advocate" (like Jesus, an advocate for the truth), "the Spirit of truth":

> *"... I will ask the Father, and he will give you another Advocate, to be with you forever. This is the Spirit of truth ... You know him, because he abides with you, and he will be in you."* (14:15-16).

In fact, the Spirit of truth is *already* in the disciples. And after Jesus' death the Spirit of truth will teach the disciples everything:

"I have said these things to you while I am with you. But the Advocate, the Holy Spirit, whom the Father will send in my name, will teach you everything, and remind you of all that I have said to you." (14:25-26).

The Advocate will not only remind the disciples of all that Jesus has said to them, but also will go further to reveal the complete truth.

"I still have many things to say to you, but you cannot bear [to hear] them now. When the Spirit of truth comes, he will guide you into all the truth: for he will not speak on his own, but will speak whatever he hears, and he will declare to you things that are to come." (16:12-13).

God Sends People to Testify

Those who believe the truth recognize within it their personal responsibility to testify to the truth to others. In this way, they are "sent" by God to testify to the truth.

John the Baptist was sent

In the prologue to the Gospel, the author tells us that the Baptist had been sent from God to "testify to the light":

There was a man sent from God, whose name was John. He came as a witness to testify to the light, so that all might believe through him. He himself was not the light, but he came to testify to the light. (1:6-8).

What was, or is, the light to which the Baptist testified? In the prologue the author tells us that the light is "the life (eternal life) that is brought into being by the Word" (*What has come into being in it* [the Word] *was life, and the life was the light of all people. 1:3b-4*).

In his testimony the Baptist testifies to Jesus, and this testimony begins even before we leave the prologue: *John testified to him and cried out, "This was he of whom I said, 'He who comes after me ranks ahead of me because he was before me." (1:15).* In saying that Jesus comes after him, yet "was" before him, the Baptist is making a theological point - or the author is using the Baptist to make a theological point. The point is that, although Jesus was born after the Baptist chronologically, the Word, the truth which constituted Jesus' being, "was" before the Baptist. It had been "in the beginning."

The prologue prepares us to find the Baptist testifying to Jesus in the main narrative portion of the Gospel. And, in fact, the main narrative begins with the Baptist's testimony to Jesus (*This is the testimony given by John ...1:19*). First, John tells the authorities who have come to question him that he is not the Messiah, not Elijah, and not "the prophet." Rather, he tells them, *"I am the voice of one crying out in the wilderness, 'Make straight the way of the Lord.'"...* (1:23). John then announces that *"Among you stands one whom you do not know, the one who is coming after me; I am not worthy to untie the thong of his sandal."* (1:26-28). And on the following day, upon seeing Jesus approaching, the Baptist declares,

> *"Here is the lamb of God who takes away the sin of the world! This is he of whom I said, 'After me comes a man who ranks ahead of me because he was before me.' I myself did not know him; but I came baptizing with water for this reason, that he might be revealed to Israel."* (1:29-31).

John understood that he had been sent to reveal Jesus to Israel and to testify that Jesus was "the Son of God":

> *And John testified, "I saw the Spirit descending from heaven like a dove, and it remained on him. I myself did not know him, but the one who sent me to baptize with water said to me, 'He on whom you see the Spirit descend and remain is the one who baptizes with the Holy Spirit.' And <u>I myself have seen and have testified that this is the Son of God.</u>"* (1:32-34).

Jesus is the focus of the Baptist's testimony in the Gospel of John, and it might be tempting to think of the Baptist as having testified to Jesus, while Jesus had testified to the truth. But in the main narrative, Jesus tells his listeners that the Baptist had also testified to the truth: *"You sent messengers to John, and he testified to the truth. ... He was a burning lamp, and you were willing to rejoice for a while in his light."* (5:33-35). The Baptist had testified to the truth, and he was "a burning lamp," a "light," in which Jesus' listeners had rejoiced for a while. The distinction that is made between Jesus and the Baptist is one of degree: *"But I have a testimony greater than John's. ..."* (5:36).

Jesus was sent

Jesus refers to his having been sent by God throughout the Gospel of John. Immediately after having recognized John the Baptist for his role in testifying to the truth, Jesus claims, *"The works that the Father has given me to complete, the very works that I am doing, testify on my behalf that the Father has sent me."* (5:36b). Other instances include:

"My food is to do the will of him who sent me and to complete his work." (4:34),

"... I have come down from heaven, not to do my own will, but the will of him who sent me." (6:38),

"... My teaching is not mine but his who sent me." (7:16),

*"... I came from God and now I am here. I did not
come on my own, but <u>he sent me</u>."*(8:42), and

*Then Jesus cried aloud: "Whoever believes in me
believes not in me but in <u>him who sent me</u>. And
whoever sees me sees <u>him who sent me</u>."* (12:44-
45).

Jesus understood that he had been sent to testify to the
truth: *"For this I was born, and for this <u>I came into the
world, to testify to the truth</u>."* (18:37). And, in testifying
to the truth, Jesus would be doing the will of God (6:38)
and completing[25] his work (4:34).

Unnamed colleagues of Jesus were sent

Jesus did not work alone. He worked alongside
colleagues who also had come to know the truth, and who
also had testified: *"Very truly, I tell you, <u>we speak of what
we know and testify to what</u> we <u>have seen</u>; yet you do not
receive <u>our</u> testimony.* (3:11) Although the Gospel does
not explicitly say so, it is reasonable to think of Jesus'
colleagues as having been sent to testify because, having

---

[25] Apparently what Jesus meant in verse 4:34 is that to work *toward*
completing God's work was what sustained him, not that he had
completed, or had expected to complete, God's work - for later in the
Gospel, Jesus tells his disciples: *"I still have many things to say to
you, but you cannot bear them now. When the Spirit of truth comes,
he will guide you into all the truth; for he will not speak on his own,
but will speak whatever he hears, and will declare to you the things
that are to come."* (16:12-13).

come to know and see the truth, that is what they then do - they speak and testify.

The Son was sent

The Son was also sent. In John's Gospel Jesus often speaks of himself in the third person - sometimes as "the Son of God," sometimes as "the Son of Man," and sometimes simply as "the Son." That all three terms refer to the same person is made clear in the following passage, in which we find Jesus using them interchangeably:

> *"Very truly, I tell you, the hour is coming, and is now here, when the dead will hear the voice of the Son of God, and those who hear will live. For just as the Father has life in himself, so he has granted the Son also to have life in himself; and he has given him authority to execute judgment, because he is the Son of Man. (5:25-27).*

The Son *is* the Son of God *is* the Son of Man.

The Son had been sent into the world so that those who believe in him might not perish but have eternal life, and so that the world might be saved through him:

> *"For God so loved the world that he gave his only Son, so that everyone who believes in him may not perish but may have eternal life. Indeed, God did not send the Son into the world to condemn the*

world, but in order that the world might be saved through him." (3:16-17).

This passage tells us that the Son was given so that everyone who believes in him may have eternal life and that the world might be saved through him. How was the Son to make these things happen? By testifying. The dead[26] will come to life as a result of hearing the "voice of the Son of God": *"Very truly, I tell you, the hour is coming, and is now here, when the dead will hear the voice of the Son of God, and those who hear will live."* (5:25). The Son will provide the "food" that endures for eternal life (*"Do not work for the food that perishes, but for the food that endures for eternal life, which the Son of Man will give you."* 6:27). This food is "the bread of God" (*"The bread of God is that which comes down from heaven and gives life to the world"* 6:33). It is the "bread" distributed by Jesus at the feeding of the five thousand, the truth to which he testified.

The one who comes from above was sent

The one who has come from above - that is, anyone who has come to know and to believe the truth - is thereby sent to testify to the truth, and does so:

---

[26] In the Gospel of John, the expression, "the dead," refers not to people who are dead in the literal, i.e., the material, sense, but rather to people who are dead in a figurative sense, such that they are "dead" to (alienated from or opposed to) the truth. The Gospel's use of the terms "life" and "death" will be addressed in more detail in Chapter 5 ("Life" and "Death").

The one who comes from above is above all; the one who is of the earth belongs to the earth and speaks about earthly things. The one who comes from heaven is above all. He testifies to what he has seen and heard, yet no one accepts his testimony. ... He whom God has sent speaks the words of God, for he gives the Spirit without measure. (3:31-34).

In this passage, "the one who comes from above" *is* "the one who comes from heaven" *is* "he whom God has sent." He testifies to what he has seen and heard, that is, to the truth.

The disciples were sent

Jesus' disciples also were sent. In the story of the healing of the man "blind from birth" (verses 9:1-41), Jesus and his disciples happen to walk past a man who had been born blind. The disciples ask who has sinned such that the man was born blind - the blind man or his parents? Jesus replies that neither the blind man nor his parents had sinned. Rather, the man had been born blind so that God's works might be revealed in him.

We will address *how* God's works might be revealed in the blind man later in this chapter. Here what is most relevant is what Jesus tells his disciples next. In the NRSV translation, Jesus tells his disciples, *"We must work the works of him who sent <u>me</u> while it is day; night* *is coming when no one can work."* (9:4). In a footnote, the NRSV mentions that "other ancient authorities" [other ancient copies of the Gospel] read *us"* (rather than "me"). What the footnote does not acknowledge is that these other ancient authorities are in fact the earliest. Thus, the Gospel appears to have originally said, *"We must work the works of him who sent <u>us</u> ...."* If so (and I believe it is so), it was Jesus' understanding that his disciples had also been sent by God to do God's works.

What are "the works of him who sent us?" God reveals the truth to Jesus and sends Jesus to testify to others. Jesus then reveals the truth to his disciples and sends them to testify. This is how he puts it to God the Father in his intercessory prayer on behalf of the disciples,

> *"<u>I have given them your word</u>, and the world has hated them because they do not belong to the world, just as I do not belong to the world ... Sanctify them in the truth; your word is truth. <u>As you have sent me into the world, so I have sent them into the world</u>. And for their sakes I sanctify myself, so that they may also be sanctified in truth.* (17:14-19).

Jesus sent the disciples during his natural life in this world. But in case the disciples have missed the point, he sends them again after his death.[27] During an appearance

---

[27] I purposely avoid using the term "resurrection" in connection with

to some of his disciples[28] the author tells us, *Jesus said to them, "Peace be with you. As the Father sent me, so I send you."* (20:21-22).

The man born blind was sent

The process of one's coming to know the truth and then accepting one's responsibility to testify to the truth can be seen in the story of Jesus' healing of a man born blind. The story begins,

> As he [Jesus] *walked along, he saw a man blind from birth. His disciples asked him, "Rabbi, who sinned, this man or his parents, that he was born blind?"* (9:1-2).

The disciples' question presumes that being born blind is evidence of sin - a sin committed by the blind man or by his parents. Jesus rejects his disciples' assumption and declares that the man was born blind, *not* because of sin, but so that God's works might be revealed in him (the blind man):

Jesus' after-death appearances because to Jesus, as he is represented in the Gospel, the resurrection is something that happens (if it does) during a person's natural lifetime in this world. I will discuss this issue in more detail in Chapter 5 (The Meaning of Life).

[28] After his death, Jesus appears to Mary Magdalene and sends her to tell his "brothers" (his male disciples) that he is ascending to the Father. She does so, and that evening Jesus appears to all of his male disciples, except Thomas. (John 20:11-19).

Jesus answered, "Neither this man nor his parents sinned; he was born blind so that God's work might be revealed in him. We must work the works of him who sent [us]²⁹ while it is day; night is coming when no one can work." (9:3-4).

In this answer, Jesus is telling the disciples - and the author is telling us - that events in this world, such as a man being born blind, are not to be viewed as occasions for assigning blame, but rather as occasions for doing God's work. To illustrate his point, Jesus immediately begins doing God's work. After saying, *"As long as I am in the world, I am the light of the world."* (9:5)," Jesus spits on the ground to make some mud, spreads the mud on the man's eyes, and tells him, *"Go, wash in the pool of Siloam" (which means sent). Then he went and washed and came back able to see. (9:7).* The phrase "which means sent" is present in the Greek text of the Gospel.

On one level, we could read the story of the man born blind as a miracle story, a story that tells us something about the Jesus - his authority and his power. But on a deeper level, we could read the story figuratively as a representation of God's work in this world. God's work is revealed in the blind man's "eyes" being opened, that is, in his coming to see the truth. The man is able to see

---

²⁹ The NRSV translation reads, "We must work the works of him who sent me ..."; however, the earliest manuscripts of the Gospel of John read ,"We must work the works of him who sent us ..." . I have chosen the "us" reading because of its earlier date and because it is a better fit with the theme of being sent in the story that follows.

when he washes in the pool of Siloam. In what might appear to be an incidental comment, the author tells us that the name of the pool (Siloam) means "sent." But his comment is a clue to the deeper meaning of the story. When the "mud" (ignorance or misunderstanding of the truth) is removed, the "blind man" (blind to the truth) "sees" (understands and recognizes the truth).

Now that he has seen the truth, the born blind man is almost unrecognizable by his neighbors:

The neighbors and those who had seen him before as a beggar began to ask, "Is this not the man who used to sit and beg? Some were saying, "It is he." Others were saying, "No, but it is someone like him." (9:8-9).

Now that he knows the truth the man blind from birth can no longer merely sit and beg; he must get up and testify to the truth. And this is just what we find him doing throughout the rest of the story. The man is brought before the Pharisees for questioning, but the Pharisees fall to arguing among themselves about whether Jesus is a sinner or a man of God. So they turn to the blind man and ask him, *"What do you say about him? It was your eyes he opened."*, and the man born blind answers, *"He is a prophet."* (9:17). By declaring that Jesus is a prophet (one who speaks for God) the blind man is endorsing Jesus' testimony to the truth, and adding his own testimony to it. The Pharisees call the man before them for a second time, and this time they argue, *"We know that God has spoken to Moses, but as for this man [Jesus] we do not know where he comes from."* (9:29). At this point, the man born blind testifies again to Jesus, and indirectly to the truth that he represented:

> *"Here is an astonishing thing! You do not know where he comes from, and yet he opened my eyes. ... Never since the world began has it been heard that anyone opened the eyes of a person born blind. If this man were not from God, he could do nothing."* (9:30-33).

God Draws People to the Truth

God not only reveals the truth to people and sends them to testify to it, he also draws people *to* the truth. In fact, John's Gospel tells us that no one can come to Jesus for the truth, *unless* they have been drawn to him by God:

> *Jesus answered them, "Do not complain among yourselves. <u>No one can come to me unless drawn by the Father who sent me</u>: and I will raise that person up on the last day. (6:44).*

Moreover, those who come to Jesus will *already* have "heard and learned" the truth from the Father:

It is written in the prophets, 'And they shall be taught by God.' Everyone who has heard and learned from the Father comes to me." (6:45).

Jesus is saying here that we don't come to know God through Jesus, but rather we come to know Jesus through God. God grants the listener access to Jesus: *"...I have told you that no one can come to me unless it is granted by the Father."* (6:65).

Earlier, Jesus had explained that those who come to him are *given to him* by God.

[All whom][30] the Father gives to me will come to me, and anyone who comes to me I will never drive away; for I have come down from heaven, not to do my own will, but the will of him who sent me. (6:37-38).

The idea that those who listen to Jesus are given to him is developed further in the next two verses of the Gospel:

---

[30] The words in brackets at the beginning of this passage represent a deviation from the NRSV translation. The original Greek is ambiguous because the noun with which 6:37 begins could be rendered as "all" or "everything," or "everyone." The NRSV translation renders the Greek as "every*thing*," thus prejudicing the sense toward the impersonal; the NIV renders it as "all," thereby preserving the ambiguity. While it is true that God gives things to Jesus (words, power, authority, power, etc.), and thus "everything" could make sense in verse 6:37, the verses that immediately follow make it clear that Jesus is speaking of "every*one*," of "all whom," in verses 6:37-38.

*And this is the will of him who sent me, that I
should lose [none]³¹ of all that he has given me,
but raise [them] up on the last day.* (6:39), and

*This is indeed the will of my Father, that all who
see the Son and believe in him may have eternal
life; and I will raise them up on the last day."*
(6:40).

Taken together, each of these verses helps us to
understand the other. For Jesus to lose none of those who
are given to him is for Jesus (as the Son) to bring those
given to him to eternal life. At the same time, those who
are given to Jesus are those who see (understand) the Son
and believe in him. And to see and believe is to have
eternal life.

Jesus returns to the idea that the audience for the truth
is given to him by God much later. In his extended prayer
of intercession on behalf of his disciples, Jesus tells God
that he has made his (God's) name known to those who
had been given to him (Jesus) from the world:

---

³¹ All modern English translations are in agreement that the final
pronoun in verse 6:40 should be read as a personal pronoun (in this
case, "them"). Consequently, I have chosen to replace the final
pronoun of the NRSV translation ("it") in verse 6:39 with a personal
pronoun ("them"). I have also chosen to change the word "nothing"
which appears earlier in the NRSV reading of 6:39 to "none" (to be
understood as "no one," rather than "no thing"), to parallel the phrase
"all who see the Son ..." in verse 6:40. The resulting translation of
6:39 is, in fact, precisely what one finds in the New International
Version (NIV).

*"I have made your name known to <u>those whom you
gave me</u> from the world. <u>They were yours, and
you gave them to me</u>, and they have kept your
word. Now they know that everything you have
given me is from you; for the words that you gave
to me I have given them, and they have received
them and know in truth that I came from you; and
they have believed that you sent me."* (17:6-8).

The same point is then made in two subsequent passages
but some English translations of these passages are so
garbled that the meaning of the Greek is lost. Alas, the
NRSV renders verses 17:11-12:

*"... Holy Father, protect them in <u>your name that
you have given me</u>, so that they may be one as we
are one. While I was with them, I protected them
in <u>your name that you have given me</u>."*

In fact, what has been given Jesus in this passage is not
his name, but rather his audience. A correct translation of
these verses would read something like this:

*"... Holy Father, protect in your name <u>those whom
you have given me</u>, so that they may all be one as
we are one. While I was with them, I protected in
your name <u>those whom you have given me</u>. ..."*

The translators of the King James Version (KJV) of the
Gospel had correctly understood the meaning of this

passage in the year 1611: "*... keep through thine own name those whom thou hast given me ...*" (17:11) and "*... I kept them in thy name: those that thou gavest me I have kept, and none of them is lost ...*" (17:12). Even earlier, in 1534, William Tyndale had realized that Jesus was referring to people who had been given to him ("*Holy father, keep in thine own name, them which thou hast given me ...*").[32]

The author of the Gospel of John (and Jesus as he is represented in the Gospel) understood that the audience for the truth was, and would continue to be, provided by God. But an even stronger claim is made in John's Gospel. It is not merely a matter of God working with, or on, people living in this world, to incline them to listen to Jesus (or more generally, to the truth). The Gospel tells us that, like Jesus, people who are able to hear the words of God have *come from* God. This point is made by Jesus during his argument with opponents about who the true descendants of Abraham are. Jesus asks his opponents why, inasmuch as he has been telling them the truth, they still don't believe him. He then supplies his own answer: "*Whoever is from God hears the words of God. The reason you do not hear them is that you are not from God.*" (8:47). To hear the truth (the words of God) one

---

[32] *Tyndale's New Testament*, Translated from the Greek by William Tynsdale in 1534, (a modern-spelling edition with introduction by David Daniell), published in 1989 by Yale University Press, New Haven and London, p. 158.

must have come from God. Or perhaps, to hear the truth
is to have come from God.

That one must have come from God in order to hear
the truth should not come as a surprise in view of what we
have already been told in the prologue to John's Gospel.
There the author tells us that *"to all who received him,
who believed in his name, he gave power to become
children of God, who were born, not of blood ... but of
God."* (1:12-13) We will return to the what the Gospel
says about the origin of the believer in Chapter 6 (Eternal
Life). For the remainder of this chapter we will continue
to focus on how God works in order to realize the purpose
behind existence.

The idea that one has a special relationship to God (or,
rather, to the truth which is God) even prior to hearing
Jesus is also expressed in terms of "belonging to" the
truth. During Jesus' arraignment Pilate asks him, *"So you
are king?"* And Jesus answers, *"You say that I am king.
For this I was born, and for this I came into the world, to
testify to the truth. Everyone who belongs to the truth
listens to my voice."* (18:37).

God Participates in the Individual's Response
to the Truth

God reveals the truth directly to individuals, sends
them to testify to the truth, and draws people to the truth.
God does these things in order to recruit people for the

task of bringing love into being, of infusing this otherwise merely material world with love. For one to actually *be* an agent of God, he or she must both believe *and* bring his or her life into accord with the truth. In the Gospel of John, God as himself, the Spirit, and divine grace is represented as participating in each step of the process.

The work of God

During his "bread of life" discourse (shortly after the feeding of the five-thousand with loaves and fishes) Jesus tells the crowd that has found him in Capernaum that they are following him, not because of "signs" that he has given them, but because of the "loaves" which they have eaten. Jesus then urges his listeners, *"Do not work for the food that perishes but for the food that endures for eternal life, which the Son of Man will give you. For it is on him that God the Father has set his seal"* (6:27). The people then ask, *"What must we do to perform the works of God"?* (6:28). Although the people ask what *they* must do, Jesus tells them what *God* does: *"This is the work of God, that you believe in him whom he has sent."* (6:29) Jesus' answer is responsive if we think of our coming to believe as simultaneously our work *and* the work of God. God's work is to be done by us.

The work of the Spirit

How is it that one comes to believe the truth? And how is it that a person who believes decides to bring his or her life into accord with the truth? There is no way to account for these things happening. Jesus attributes their happening to the "the Spirit." In his conversation with Nicodemus, early in the Gospel, Jesus explains how it is that a person can see or enter into the kingdom of God, *"Do not be astonished that I said to you, 'You must be born from above.'* <u>*The wind blows where it chooses, and you hear the sound of it, but you do not know where it comes from or where it goes. So it is with anyone born of the Spirit.*</u>*"* (3:7-8). This was Jesus' way of saying that being able to "see" (recognize) and to "enter" (participate in) the kingdom of God cannot be accounted for without attribution to a transcendent influence. In this passage, the Gospel attributes our coming to believe, and to bring our lives into accord with the truth (see and enter the kingdom) to the work of the Spirit.

Grace

God's involvement at every step in the reception and appropriation of the truth is encompassed by the concept of "grace." In the Gospel, the word "grace," appears only in the prologue, where we find:

> *And the Word became flesh and lived among us, and we have seen his glory, the glory as of a father's only son, full of grace and truth. .... <u>From his fullness we have all received, grace upon grace. The law indeed was given through Moses; grace and truth came through Jesus Christ</u>.* (1:14-17).

In this passage, the Greek word translated as grace can mean a gift, favor, or reward. The author is telling his early readers (and listeners) that through Jesus they have received a gift from God. It isn't possible to account for a person, perhaps for oneself, coming to recognize the truth and deciding to take it to heart solely by reference to the things of this world. It can be accounted for only by reference to a transcendent influence, to God, to the truth.

Somewhat surprisingly, after its brief appearance in the prologue, the word "grace" does not appear again in the Gospel. This is not to say that the phenomenon isn't represented; what we might think of as grace is subsumed within the "works" of God.

Observations on God's *Modus Operandi*

As the author of the Gospel of John understood it (and Jesus as he is represented in the Gospel understood it), God works to realize the purpose behind existence by revealing the truth to individuals, sending them to testify to the truth, and telling them what to say. God also draws people to the truth, and participates in their coming to know - and to bring their lives into accord with - the truth.

Unfortunately this traditional, causal way of speaking about how God works could seem to suggest that existence is a cosmic puppet show, with God as puppet master who pulls all the strings. And representing God as a person could suggest the possibility that God might say or do just anything. Nothing could be further from the truth. God does not control everything that happens in this world. Moreover, God cannot say and do just anything. Whatever God says or does must be compatible with, and an expression of, the truth - as should everything that we say about God.

An alternative, and less problematic, way of speaking about how God works would be to replace the word "God" with "the truth." Thus, we could say, *the truth* realizes *its* purpose - the purpose behind existence - by revealing *itself* to individuals, sending them to testify to the truth, and telling them what to say. *The truth* also draws people to itself, and participates in their coming to believe, and to bring their lives into accord with, the truth.

The switch to this impersonal way of speaking reduces the likelihood of our misunderstanding or misrepresenting God, but it does not address the issue of control vs. personal freedom and responsibility. The likelihood of thinking of ourselves as mere puppets in a meaningless play could be eliminated if we were to move from a causal to a non-causal representation of how God works. Thus, instead of saying that God reveals the truth to people, we could say simply that the truth occurs to (or dawns on) people. And instead of saying that God sends people to testify to the truth, we could say that people recognize within the truth their personal responsibility to embody and testify to the truth, and they do so.

To say that God does something is to recognize that it (the something) happens and, at the same time, recognize in its happening a manifestation of the transcendent, of the truth behind existence. In either way of speaking, what makes the realization of the purpose behind existence possible in our lives, and in the world at large, is that the truth exists - that there is a purpose behind existence. We - at least some of us, perhaps all of us when at our best - are drawn to the truth, we listen for it, we recognize the truth when we hear it, and we work to manifest the truth in our lives.

It is important to note that the truth, as it is represented in the Gospel of John, does not represent God as operating in any other way. The truth is that God does not bring down floods, fires, or any sorts of punishment on us in order to correct our behavior. To do so would be contrary to his nature or the purpose that he represents. God does *not* preordain or control events in this world. And not *everything* that happens in this world represents God's will. God *does* have a plan, but that plan is simply to reveal the truth to us, and depend on us to do our part in bringing love into being.

In Chapters 2 through 4, we have established who God is - as he is represented in the Gospel of John. In particular, we have established the nature and existence of God, God's purpose, and how it is that God works to realize his purpose. Next, in Chapters 5 through 7, we will examine what the Gospel tells us about who *we* are.

We will then continue on to what we need to become the person we are meant to be (Chapters 8-10) and what constitutes "salvation" (Chapter 11). The truth to which Jesus testified (as understood by the author of the Gospel of John) will be summarized, and the questions raised in Chapter 1 will be answered, in Chapter 12 (The Truth Is).

Points to Keep in Mind

- **God (the truth) works through people in this world to realize his (its) ultimate purpose - the bringing of love into being. He does so by revealing the truth to individuals, sending them to testify to the truth, and telling them what to say and do.**

- **God draws people to the truth and participates both in their recognition of the truth and in their decision to bring their lives into accord with the truth.**

- **Alternatively, we could say that sometimes the truth occurs to people. They recognize within the truth their personal responsibility to love and to testify to the truth to others, and they do so.**

- **God does not operate in any other way. God does not send down floods, fires, plagues, or other types of punishment on us in order to**

correct our behavior. God does not preordain
or control events in this world.

- God has a "plan" to realize his purpose, the
  purpose behind existence. That plan is simply
  to reveal the truth to us, and rely on us to do
  our part in bringing love into being.

Chapter 5

LIFE AND DEATH

"Very truly, I tell you, anyone who hears my word and believes him who sent me has eternal life, and does not come under judgment, but has passed from death to life." (5:24)

The truth, as it is represented in the Gospel of John, encompasses not only who God is, but also who *we* are. Or perhaps it would be better to say, who we are *meant to be*. In the first four verses of the Gospel, the author tells us that *all things* have come into being through the Word. He then focuses our attention on *one* thing in particular, "life":

In the beginning was the Word ... All things came into being through it [the Word][33] *and without it not one thing came into being. <u>What has come into being in it was life</u> ....* (1:1-4).

That we might come to have life is a central concern of the Gospel of John. In the main narrative, Jesus - or perhaps it is the author[34] - tells us that God's purpose in

---

[33] Here again, and throughout this book, I translate the Greek pronouns in this passage as neuter (it) so as to best fit the noun (logos) to which they refer. Most translations render these pronouns as masculine (him) under the mistaken impression that they refer to Jesus , who has not yet been mentioned in the text.

[34] The NRSV translation notes that "Some interpreters hold that the

107

having sent his Son into the world was that believers in "his only Son" might come to have eternal life (*"For God so loved the world that he gave his only Son, so that everyone who believes in him may not perish but may have eternal life."* 3:16). In this verse, Jesus uses the expression "eternal life" rather than simply "life," but this is a distinction without a difference as "life" and "eternal life" often are used interchangeably in John's Gospel. This can be seen in verse 5:24, in which Jesus tells his listeners, *"Very truly, I tell you, anyone who hears my word and believes him who sent me has <u>eternal life</u>, and does not come under judgment, but has passed from death to <u>life</u>."*

Jesus understood that he had come to testify to the truth so that people might come to have life (*" ... I came that they* [those who listen to him] *may have life, and have it abundantly."* 10:10). And this was the author's purpose in writing his Gospel:

> *Now Jesus did many other signs in the presence of his disciples ... <u>these are written so that you may come to believe</u> that Jesus is the Messiah, the Son of God, <u>and that through believing you may have life</u> in his name.* 20:30-31).

---

quotation concludes with verse 3:15," as does the NIV. If so, then verses 3:16-21 could be the words of the author, as verses 3:22-25 clearly are. The NAB ends the quote at verse 3:15; the NASB continues the quote past verse 16; and the KJV, RNT and AB do not use quotation marks at all.

Life and Death

Why life? Why did God, and Jesus, and the author of the Gospel want us to have eternal life? I am inclined to believe that they did so because in coming to have eternal life we would recognize our personal responsibility to love others (see Part III, What We Are Meant to Be Doing, Chapters 8-10). In loving others we would contribute to realizing the purpose behind existence: the bringing of love into this world. Toward this end we are the intended recipients of life, eternal life.

The Meaning of "Life"

What did the author of the Gospel, and Jesus as he is represented in the Gospel, mean by "life," that is, by eternal life? Some basic points about eternal life are suggested in verse 5:24. These are:

- A person comes to have eternal life through belief, through believing the truth to which Jesus testified (*"Very truly I tell you, <u>anyone who hears my word</u> [the truth] <u>and believes him who sent me</u> [God or, equivalently, the truth] <u>has eternal life</u> ... "*),

- A person comes to have eternal life in the here and now, that is, during his or her lifetime in this world (*"... <u>anyone who hears my word and believes him who sent me has eternal life, and</u> ... <u>has</u> passed from death to life."*), and

109

Eternal life comes to those who are already alive in the literal sense. Otherwise they would be in no condition to hear and believe. Accordingly, life in the eternal sense is to be understood not literally but rather figuratively. Similarly, inasmuch as the already living recipient of eternal life is said to have passed "from death to life," it should be clear that "death" is also meant to be understood figuratively.

Eternal life in the here and now

Verse 5:24 tells us that anyone who hears and believes "has" eternal life, and "has passed" from death to life. There is no suggestion here of a person coming to have eternal life in the future. However, the verse that immediately follows does speak of people coming to have life in the future (*"Very truly, I tell you, the hour is coming, and is now here, when the dead will hear the voice of the Son of God, and those who hear will live"*) (5:25). But in this verse, the coming into possession of life occurs in the future because the hearing of "the voice of the Son of God" also occurs in the future. In other words, the coming to have life occurs contemporaneously with "hearing" the Son of God's "voice." It should be pointed out that in this context "hearing" encompasses not merely registering the sounds of the voice of the Son of God, but also understanding, and recognizing the truth of, what he is saying.

The conclusion that those who believe Jesus come to have eternal life in the here and now - during their natural lifetimes in this, the material world - is also supported by other verses in the Gospel. Verse 3:36 tells us, *Whoever believes in the Son has* [present tense] *eternal life; whoever disobeys the Son will not* [future tense] *see life, but must endure God's wrath.* The author could have said, "Whoever believes in the Son *will have* eternal life ...," but didn't. He did say, however, that whoever *disobeys* the Son will *not* see life. Here, the author switches to the future tense – and it might be tempting to think that his use of the present tense in the first clause might have been a mistake. But there are too many other instances in which life is spoken of as coming into being in the present (or even the past) tense for it to have been a mistake. A more likely reason for the future tense for disbelievers in verse 3:36 is that the author is saying it will not only *not* happen in the present, but will never happen at all, unless the person brings his or her behavior into accord with the truth.

Additional support can be found in verse 6:47 where we are once again told that those who believe already possess eternal life: *"Very truly, I tell you, whoever believes has eternal life."* And only a few verses later, employing "flesh" and "blood" as metaphors for the truth, we find Jesus saying,

> *"Very truly, I tell you, unless you eat the flesh of the Son of Man and drink his blood, you have no*

life in you. <u>Those who eat my flesh and drink my</u>
<u>blood have eternal life</u>, and I will raise them up on
the last day ... " (6:53-54).

Here we are told that those[35] who "consume" Jesus' flesh
and his blood (receive and digest the truth) already *have*
(present tense) eternal life. But what are we to make of
the clause, "and I will raise them up on the last day"?
Being raised up is said to occur "on the last day," but is
being raised up the same thing as coming to have eternal
life? The "and" at the beginning of the clause allows for
the possibility that being raised up is something different
from coming to have eternal life. But it isn't. To come to
have eternal life *is* to be raised up, but "on the last day"
need not be read as a temporal reference. More likely it
has a meaning similar to "at the end of the day," or "when
all is said and done."

"Life" comes to the living

That eternal life would come to the already living is
just what one would expect. After all, Jesus testified -
and the author of the Gospel wrote - to the living in the
expectation that they might come to have eternal life.
Clearly, "life" comes to the living. But is this always the
case? Some passages in the Gospel might seem to be

---

[35] The Greek at this point actually says, "the one feeding on my flesh
and drinking my blood has eternal life." This is perhaps even clearer
about the point that one has eternal life in the here and now, and also
better reflects the fact that coming to have eternal life is something
that happens at the individual rather than the collective level.

saying that even the dead will hear Jesus' voice and come to have life. In verse 5:25 we find Jesus saying, *"Very truly, I tell you, the hour is coming, and is now here, when* <u>*the dead will hear the voice of the Son of God, and those*</u> <u>*who hear will live.*</u>*"* But who are "the dead" in this verse? And in what sense are they dead?

When Jesus spoke of people passing "from death to life," and when he announced that the hour had come "when the dead would hear the voice of the Son of God and live," he realized that his words would startle his listeners. But, rather than clarify his meaning, Jesus chooses to dig even deeper:

> *"Do not be astonished at this; for the hour is coming when* <u>*all who are in their graves*</u> *will hear his [the Son of God's] voice and will* <u>*come out*</u> *—* *those who have done good, to the resurrection of life, and those who have done evil, to the resurrection of condemnation."* (5:28-29).

In their graves! Those who will be brought to life (or to condemnation) are not only dead, but in their graves. And yet they will come out!

Were Jesus' listeners (and are the Gospel's readers) meant to believe that Jesus' voice would be heard by people who are literally dead, and in their graves? And are we to believe that they will come bodily out of their graves? There is no reason to believe so. A more likely meaning of Jesus' words – and the only meaning that is compatible with the Gospel as a whole – is that the "graves" to which Jesus refers are figurative graves - but no less real for being figurative. I am inclined to think of these graves as being constructed of people's (our) attachments to the values and things of this world, and by their (our) resultant alienation from the truth.

Would Jesus have employed figurative language in this way, and to this extent? Yes. And, if the Gospel has it right, he did.

Jesus' Use of Figurative Language

Jesus employs figurative language throughout the Gospel of John. Some particularly prominent instances of his use of figurative language involve references to: the "bread from heaven," Jesus' "flesh" and his "blood," Jesus as "shepherd" and "gate," and the disciples in "childbirth."

The bread from heaven

In Chapter 6 of the Gospel Jesus' listeners ask him what sign he can give them, so that they might believe him. And, as an example of what they are looking for, they point to the "manna," the "bread from heaven" that their ancestors had been given in the wilderness. Jesus' then enters into the following exchange with his listeners:

*"Very truly, I tell you, it was not Moses who gave
you the bread from heaven, it is my Father who
gives you the true bread from heaven. For the
bread of God is that which comes down from
heaven and gives life to the world." They said to
him, "Sir, give this bread to us always." Jesus
said to them, "I am the bread of life. Whoever
comes to me will never be hungry, and whoever
believes in me will never be thirsty." (6:32-35).*

What is the "bread from heaven," the "true bread, " the
"bread of God … which comes down from heaven and
gives life to the world"? The "bread" of which Jesus
speaks in verses 6:32-35 is the Word, the word of God,
the truth to which Jesus testified. Those who come to
Jesus and believe in him will no longer hunger or thirst
for it.

Why bread? Just as bread must be eaten - consumed
and digested in order for it to nourish the body - so too the
truth must be heard and understood in order for it to bring
a person to eternal life. And so it is not surprising to find
Jesus also employing "eating" as a metaphor for a
person's reception of the Word:

*"I am the bread of life. Your ancestors ate the
manna in the wilderness, and they died. This is
the bread that comes down from heaven, so that
one may eat of it and not die. I am the living
bread that came down from heaven. Whoever eats*

of this bread will live forever; and the bread that I will give for the life of the world is my flesh. (6:48-51).

Whoever "eats" the "bread" that Jesus represents will live forever.

Jesus' flesh and blood

At the end of the last passage, Jesus speaks of the "bread" being his "flesh." It is improbable in the extreme that Jesus is referring here to his flesh in a literal sense. After all, as he points out just a few verses later, the flesh is useless: *"It is the spirit that gives life; the flesh is useless ...."* (6:63). The "flesh" spoken of in verses 6:48-51 is the Word, the "bread" that comes down from heaven. It is this metaphorical flesh that constitutes Jesus' true and transcendent self. And, not surprisingly, this "flesh" must be "eaten " (consumed and digested) for one to have eternal life.

Jesus' figurative use of language is largely lost on his listeners: *The Jews then disputed among themselves, saying, "How can this man give us his flesh to eat?"* (6:52). Rather than clarify his meaning, Jesus compounds his listeners' confusion by informing them that they must also drink his blood:

So Jesus said to them, "Very truly, I tell you, unless you eat the flesh of the Son of Man and

drink his blood, you have no life in you. Those
who eat my flesh and drink my blood have eternal
life, and I will raise them up on the last day; for
my flesh is true food and my blood is true drink.
Those who eat my flesh and drink my blood abide
in me, and I in them. ...whoever eats me will live
because of me. This is the bread that came down
from heaven, not like that which your ancestors
ate, and they died. But the one who eats this
bread will live forever." He said these things
while he was teaching in the synagogue at
Capernaum. (6:53-59).

Jesus' explanation was not well received. Even many of
his own disciples found his teaching difficult to accept:
When many of his disciples heard it, they said, "This
teaching is difficult; who can accept it?" (6:60).

What are *we* to make of what Jesus said about his
flesh and his blood? Did he expect anyone to literally eat
his flesh and drink his blood? Of course not. His
teaching here is another metaphorical way of saying that,
in order to have eternal life, a person will need to hear,
understand, and take to heart the truth to which he was
testifying.

Jesus as the good shepherd, and the gate

The author of the Gospel comments on Jesus' use of
figurative speech in what has been referred to as "the

good shepherd discourse." In this discourse, or sermon, Jesus tries to explain what he has been doing by likening his role to that of a shepherd:

> *"The one who enters by the gate is the shepherd of the sheep. The gatekeeper* [God] *opens the gate for him* [the shepherd], *and the sheep hear his* [the shepherd's] *voice. He calls his own sheep by name and leads them out. When he has brought out all his own, he goes ahead of them, and the sheep follow him because they know his voice. They will not follow a stranger, but they will run from him because they do not know the voice of strangers."* (10:2-5).

The author then tells the readers, *Jesus used this figure of speech with them, but they did not understand what he was saying to them.* (10:6) Here too, in spite of his listeners' lack of understanding, Jesus continues to employ figurative language, telling his listeners that he is both "the gate" (*So again Jesus said to them, "Very truly, I tell you, I am the gate for the sheep."* 10:7)[36] and "the good shepherd (*"I am the good shepherd. The good shepherd lays down his life for the sheep."* 10:11).

---

[36] One early "witness" (ancient manuscript of the Gospel) reads, "I am the shepherd," instead of, "I am the gate," in verse 10:7 and thus maintains the continuity of the metaphor throughout the discourse.

Life and Death

The disciples in childbirth

Toward the end of the Gospel, in what can be thought of as his farewell address to his disciples, Jesus tells them: *"A little while, and you will no longer see me, and again a little while, and you will see me.* 16:16). The disciples are puzzled by this statement and ask themselves what Jesus means. Jesus, although aware of their difficulty in understanding his words nevertheless goes on to tell the disciples that they will weep and mourn while the world rejoices; they will have pain, but their pain will turn to joy. He then likens the disciples' predicament to that of a woman in labor, who will forget her former anguish once her child is born (*"When a woman is in labor, she has pain, because her hour has come. But when her child is born, she no longer remembers the anguish because of the joy of having brought a human into the world."* (16:21). And he speaks of the joy they will experience when they see him again: *"So you have pain now; but I will see you again, and your hearts will rejoice, and no one will take your joy from you.* (16:22).

Having said all these things, Jesus explicitly acknowledges that he has been using figurative language: *"I have said these things to you in figures of speech. The hour is coming when I will no longer speak to you in figures, but will tell you plainly of the Father."* (16:25). In this verse Jesus reveals not only that he has been speaking figuratively, but also that he will only begin to speak plainly of God the Father at some time in the future, in an "hour that is coming."

Life and death, bread and eating, flesh and blood, sheep and shepherds. Jesus employs everyday language figuratively throughout the Gospel. Consequently, when we come upon a puzzling or seemingly outrageous statement in the text, we should not assume that his words were meant to be taken literally - or that to take them literally would be the most respectful approach to understanding them. In many instances - and particularly when it matters most - Jesus words were and still are meant to be read figuratively, and *only* figuratively.

In verses 5:28-29 we are told that those who will hear the Son's voice will "come out" - some to the resurrection of life, some to the resurrection of condemnation. To "come out" to the resurrection of life is just another way of saying that these people will "pass from death to life. The expression "come out" is used again later in the Gospel, in the story of the raising of Lazarus. This story will tell us more about what the author, and/or Jesus, meant by life and death.

The Raising of Lazarus

The story of the raising of Lazarus begins, *Now a certain man was ill, Lazarus of Bethany ...* (11:1). Lazarus' sisters, Mary and Martha, send a message to Jesus saying, *"Lord, he whom you love is ill."* (11:3).

Upon receiving their message Jesus exclaims, *"This illness does not lead to death, rather it is for God's glory ..."* (11:4). Thus, at the outset, we are led to believe that Lazarus is ill, that his illness is not life threatening, and that his illness will in some way contribute to God's glory.

Perhaps because Lazarus' illness is not serious, Jesus waits two days before inviting his disciples to accompany him to Bethany. The disciples question Jesus' intention to go despite the threats that have been made against his life, but Jesus persists in going, and tells the disciples that Lazarus has only fallen asleep (*"Our friend Lazarus has fallen asleep, but I am going there to awaken him."* 11:11). The disciples accept this new information and say to Jesus, *"Lord, if he has fallen asleep, he will be all right."* (11:12). At this point the author comments: *Jesus, however, had been speaking about his* [Lazarus'] *death, but they thought he was referring merely to sleep.* (11:13). Jesus now tells his disciples, *"Lazarus is dead."* (11:14).

The disciples (and we) have been told first that Lazarus is ill, then asleep, and finally, dead. Either his health had been declining rapidly (and Jesus somehow knew that it had), or Jesus was once again employing figurative language. If so, Lazarus' condition could be described figuratively using any or all of the terms: "ill," "asleep," or "dead." One of Jesus' disciples, Thomas, seems to have recognized this possibility, for he invites his fellow disciples to "die" with Lazarus, *"Let us also*

121

go, that we may die with him." (11:16). This is not something a person would be likely to say if the person thought that he or she would die in the literal sense. However, it *is* something a person might say if he or she understood Jesus' words figuratively, perhaps meaning to "die" to the things of this world, so as to facilitate the person's coming to have life, eternal life.

In any case, on the way to Bethany Jesus meets and talks with Martha, who laments her brother's death (*"Lord, if you had been here, my brother would not have died"* 11:21). She then expresses her hope that Jesus will still be able to do something (*"But even now I know that God will give you whatever you ask of him."* 11:22).

At last Jesus arrives at the cave in which Lazarus has been buried and tells those present to remove the stone that has been placed over the opening. At this point, Martha comments on the stench resulting from Lazarus' having been dead now for four days. But Jesus is not put off, and after some preliminary remarks he looks upward, thanks God, and cries out in a loud voice, "Lazarus, come out!" And Lazarus comes out:

> *The dead man came out, his hands and feet bound with strips of cloth, and his face wrapped in a cloth. Jesus said to them, "Unbind him, and let him go."* (11:44).

The raising of Lazarus is a particularly dramatic story. Jesus raises a person from the dead, and merely by issuing a command! What are we to make of this story? Did the author intend that we take it literally? Did he intend that we think of Lazarus as having been literally dead for four days and then having been brought bodily back to life?

There are certain features of the story that make it seem as if the author could have meant us to read it literally. Jesus' direct statement (in verse 11:14) that Lazarus is dead certainly allows for Lazarus being literally dead. And a literal interpretation is invited by the realistic details that are included in the story: the delays in getting to Bethany, the stench from the tomb, the strips of cloth binding Lazarus' hands and feet. Moreover, we can imagine a motive for the author wanting us to take the story literally. Taken literally, the story could be read as confirming Jesus' power and his authority. Who but one sent by God could perform such a feat? Thus, there are reasons to believe that we should take the story of the raising of Lazarus literally. But there are stronger reasons to believe that the author did not intend us to take the story literally.

Jesus' conversation with Martha

One reason to believe that we are *not* meant to take the story of the raising of Lazarus literally has to do with the content of a conversation between Jesus and Martha in the story. I passed over this conversation in my overview of the story. But it is the content of their conversation that reveals the point of the story in which it is embedded - and undermines the notion that the author wanted us to believe that Lazarus was literally raised from the dead. The conversation begins with Martha telling Jesus that if he had been present her brother would not have died, and expressing her confidence that Jesus might still prevail upon God to do something. The conversation continues,

> *Jesus said to her, "Your brother will rise again."*
> *Martha said to him, "I know that he will rise*
> *again in the resurrection on the last day." Jesus*
> *said to her, "I am the resurrection and the life.*
> *Those who believe in me, even though they die,*
> *will live, and everyone who lives and believes in*
> *me will never die. Do you believe this?" She said*
> *to him, "Yes, Lord, I believe that you are the*
> *Messiah, the Son of God, the one coming into the*
> *world." (11:23-27).*

At first glance this passage might seem to be compatible with an understanding that Lazarus was literally raised from the dead. Jesus assures Martha that her brother will rise again, and Martha replies that she knows that he will rise again - on the last day. But Jesus does not confirm Martha's statement. Instead, he tells her that *he* is the resurrection and the life, and then presents her with a riddle. The riddle is this: *"Those who believe in me, even though they die, will live, and everyone who lives and believes in me will never die." (11:25b-26a)*

Jesus is particularly interested in what Martha thinks
about what he has just said, and so he asks her bluntly,
"Do you believe this?" (11:26). Martha answers, *"Yes,
Lord, I believe that you are the Messiah, the Son of God,
the one coming into the world."* (11:27).

Martha begins by saying, "Yes," and then that she
believes Jesus to be "the Messiah, the Son of God, the one
coming into the world." Why did she do this? Jesus had
not asked Martha who she thought him to be; he had
merely asked her if she believed what he had said about
dying and yet never dying. Although Martha's confession
might seem to be out of place, it is consistent with her
"yes." To believe Jesus, to believe his testimony to the
truth, is to *in effect* recognize him as "the Messiah, the
Son of God, the one coming into the world."

What is it that Martha was to believe? How is it that a
person can die, yet never die? The key to understanding
Jesus' riddle is that a person can be alive or dead in either
(or both) of two senses: the literal (material) sense and a
figurative (transcendent) sense. And we could think of
ourselves as having two selves: a material self and a
transcendent self. Our material self comes in into being
through familiar socio-biological processes. Our
transcendent self comes into being in response to the
Word, to the truth. Although our material self will die,
our transcendent self will never die. With this
understanding in mind, this is how we might undo Jesus'
riddle: Those who believe in me, even though they die in

the material sense, will live on in the transcendent sense. And everyone who believes in me will never die (in the transcendent sense).

The solution to Jesus' riddle makes a literal interpretation of the raising of Lazarus irrelevant. The life that comes into being in response to the Word (eternal life) is not subject to death, and thus there is no need of a bodily resurrection. "Life" (eternal life) *is* resurrection, what Jesus refers to in the Gospel as "the resurrection of life":

> *"Do not be astonished at this; for <u>the hour is</u> <u>coming when all who are in their graves will hear</u> <u>his</u>* [the Son of Man's] *<u>voice and will come out -</u> <u>those who have done good, to the resurrection of</u> <u>life</u>, and those who have done evil, to the resurrection of condemnation.* (5:28-29).

And to have eternal life is to be saved from "the resurrection of condemnation" which, of course, is no resurrection at all.

The story of Lazarus within its larger context

Jesus' conversation with Martha renders any literal interpretation of the raising of Lazarus meaningless. If read literally, the story is neither illustrative of nor or consistent with, the process of coming to have life that is presented throughout the Gospel. This process involves people (Jesus, the author, future evangelists) testifying to the truth; people being drawn to the truth; people hearing and believing the truth; and people thereby coming to have eternal life.

Another reason to dismiss a literal understanding of the raising of Lazarus is that neither the author nor Jesus shows any interest in bringing dead people bodily back to life. The point of Jesus' testimony and the author's writing of the Gospel is *not* to bring those who are literally dead back to life in the flesh. After all, the flesh is useless. The point is to bring those who are alive in the literal sense to life in the eternal, the transcendent, sense.

The figurative meaning of the Lazarus story

The Lazarus story, if taken literally, is not supportive of the message of Gospel, but it is supportive if understood figuratively. This is also true of other "miracle" stories in the Gospel: the changing of water into wine at the wedding at Cana, the feeding of the five-thousand with only a few loaves of bread and fish, and the restoration of sight to the man born blind. These stories are figurative representations, respectively, for: Jesus' introduction of a new understanding of the truth that is superior to the old, his satisfying of his listeners hunger and thirst for the truth, and his enabling a person to "see" the truth for the first time.

Life and Death

The story of the raising of Lazarus is a figurative representation of the power of Jesus' words, of his teaching, on one who although loved by Jesus had been, or had become, "dead" to the truth. Lazarus' condition could be described figuratively by saying that he was ill, asleep, or dead. Early in the story, just before telling his disciples that Lazarus has fallen asleep, Jesus had said to them, *"Are there not twelve hours of daylight? Those who walk during the day do not stumble because they see the light of this world. But those who walk at night stumble, because the light is not in them."* (11:9-10). Lazarus had perhaps stumbled (the Gospel does not explicitly say so) because the light (Jesus, *"the true light which enlightens everyone"* 1:8) was not in him. Lazarus had fallen "asleep" to the truth and Jesus went to awaken him (*"Our friend Lazarus has fallen asleep; but I am going there to awaken him."* 11:11).

Martha may have been correct in saying, "my brother would not have died," if Jesus had been there earlier (verse 11:21). But the Jews who shortly thereafter say, *"Could not he who opened the eyes of a blind man have kept this man from dying?"* (11:37) are on to the same thing. This reference to the story of the man born blind is particularly appropriate because it is essentially the same story told using a different metaphor (blindness rather than death). Lazarus might not have died if Jesus had been there earlier, but then we wouldn't have had the story. Jesus calls Lazarus to "come out" just as the truth calls us to come to eternal life.

128

A figurative understanding of the Lazarus story is not a modern overlay on a story that had originally been meant to be taken literally; the figurative understanding was intended from the beginning. Literal readings of the Lazarus story are misreadings of an originally figurative representation of a transcendent event, an event that is meant to happen again and again.

The story of the raising of Lazarus is, on the surface level, so dramatic that the temptation to take it literally is irresistible for many. The attraction of a literal interpretation is particularly strong for those who are seeking a "sign" that Jesus *is* who he said he is - or, more often, who they have thought he is. But signs are not able to bring about one's understanding and recognition of the truth. One either understands what Jesus was trying to say, and recognizes it as true, and *the* truth, or one doesn't. We will return to the role (or non-role) of signs in Chapter 8 (Believing) wherein we will examine the Gospel's representation of *how* it is that we are able to know the truth.

Thus far we have addressed the centrality of "life," eternal life, to the Gospel of John, the distinction between eternal life and material life, and how and when it is that a person comes to have eternal life. What we have not addressed thus far is what eternal life *is*. The nature of eternal life will be addressed in the next chapter.

Points to Keep in Mind

- We are intended recipients of eternal life, a transcendent state of being in relation to God.

- An individual comes to have eternal life through belief in the truth. (What a person is to believe, and the basis for belief, will be addressed in Chapter 8.)

- An individual comes to have eternal life (if he or she does) in the here and now, that is, during his or her otherwise ordinary lifetime in this world.

Chapter 6

ETERNAL LIFE

"And this is eternal life, that they may know you, the only true God, and Jesus Christ whom you have sent." (17:3)

The author of the Gospel of John's understanding of what eternal life is can be determined by looking at what the Gospel says about people who have eternal life. Those who do are spoken of in the Gospel as:

- having been born of God (or, equivalently, from above),
- having come from, and been sent by, God,
- belonging to the truth,
- abiding in God,
- being in God
- being one with God,
- knowing God, and
- living eternally in God.

In this chapter, we will look into what the Gospel says about each of these attributes individually, and then address what they say about who *we* are, and who we are meant to be.

Having been born of god

In the main narrative of the Gospel, Jesus tells his listeners that to believe is to have eternal life: *"Very truly, I tell you, anyone who hears my word and believes him who sent me has eternal life, and does not come under judgment, but has passed from death to life."* (5:24). But in the prologue, the author of the Gospel tells us that to believe is to have been "born of God":

> *But to all who received him, who believed in his name, he gave power to become children of God, <u>who were born</u>, not of blood or the will of the flesh or the will of man, but <u>of God</u>.* (1:12-13)

Assuming that the Gospel is in agreement with itself - and I find that it is - it is safe to say that those who have eternal life *are* those who have been born of God.

While the author uses the expression "born of God," in speaking of the origin of those who come to have eternal life, in the main narrative Jesus uses the expression "born from above." This expression is used for the first time in Jesus' conversation with Nicodemus in, Chapter 3 of the Gospel. Nicodemus opens the conversation, *"Rabbi, we know that you are a teacher who has come from God; for no one can do these signs that you do apart from the presence of God."* (3:2). Jesus then responds by saying, *"Very truly, I tell you, no one can see the kingdom of God without <u>being born from</u>*

above." (3:3). Jesus' response might seem to be unrelated to Nicodemus' statement. After all, Nicodemus had not asked how a person could see the kingdom of God. Nevertheless, Jesus' response is relevant. The point that Jesus is making verse 3:3 is that to be able to know that he (Jesus) had come from God, a person would need to have been born from above.

Some readers may be more familiar with a translation of verse 3:3 that represents Jesus as saying that no one can see the kingdom of God without being born "again," rather than "from above." The Greek word behind the English translation at this point (in English, approximately "anothen") can mean "from above," "again," or "from the top." So, how can we know which meaning Jesus or the author of the Gospel intended in verse 3:3? To determine the author's meaning, we need to ask ourselves which meaning is most consistent with the Gospel as a whole.

Apart from the two times that the word appears in the conversation with Nicodemus, the Greek word appears in only three other verses in John's Gospel, verses 3:31, 19:11, and 19:23. In verse 3:31 the word clearly means "from above," in reference to the transcendent realm (heaven):

The one who comes from above is above all; the one who is of the earth belongs to the earth and speaks of earthly things. The one who comes from heaven is above all. (3:31).

In verse 19:11, the word is also used to mean "from above": *Jesus answered him* [Pilate], *"You would have no power over me unless it had been given you from above ...."* And in verse 19:23, it is used to mean "from the top": (*They* [the soldiers at Jesus' crucifixion] *also took his tunic; now the tunic was seamless, woven in one piece from the top.*) In *no* instance is the word used in John's Gospel to mean "again." Moreover, the *idea* of being born again does not appear in the Gospel *other than* on the lips of Nicodemus, who clearly misunderstands Jesus.

In marked contrast to the absence of support for the idea of being *born again*, the idea of being born *from above* (or, equivalently, of God or of the Spirit) can be found throughout the Gospel. In his conversation with Nicodemus, Jesus continues to stress the need to be born "from above" in order to see or to enter the kingdom of God:

Nicodemus said to him, "How can anyone be born after having grown old? Can one enter a second time into the mother's womb and be born? Jesus answered, "Very truly, I tell you, no one can enter the kingdom of God without being born of water and Spirit. ... Do not be astonished that I said to you, 'You must be born from above. The wind blows where it chooses, and you hear the sound of

it, but you do not know where it comes from or
where it goes. So it is with everyone who is <u>born</u>
<u>of the Spirit</u>." (3:4-8).

In this passage Jesus uses the terms "born from above"
and "born of the Spirit" (or of water and Spirit)
interchangeably. This practice is understandable because
"above" and "the Spirit" are both references to the same
transcendent reality that stands behind existence. In one
instance Jesus uses the expression "born of water *and*
Spirit," but the inclusion of "water" in this case is
redundant inasmuch as water is employed as a metaphor
for spirit in John's Gospel, as can be seen in the following
passage:

On the last day of the festival, the great day, while
Jesus was standing there, he cried out, "Let
anyone who is thirsty come to me, and let the one
who believes in me drink. As the scripture has
said, 'Out of the believers heart shall flow <u>rivers</u>
<u>of living water</u>.'" Now he said this about the
<u>Spirit</u>, which believers in him were to receive ....
(7:37-39).

In these verses Jesus invites his listeners to come to him
to drink from the river of living water, and by "living
water," the author of the Gospel informs us that Jesus was
referring to the Spirit. Note that Jesus saw himself as a
source of "living water" (the Spirit) to his listeners, and
he anticipated that believers would also be sources of

"living water" (the Spirit) to others. The same river is to flow through Jesus and on through the believers.

Having come from/been sent by god

Closely related to the idea of having been *born of* God is the idea of having been *sent by*, or having *come from*, God. This idea is introduced in the prologue to the Gospel, wherein the author tells us that John the Baptist was sent from God: *There was a man <u>sent from God,</u> whose name was John. He came as a witness to testify to the light...* (1:6-7). This passage tells us that the Baptist was sent *from* God - not merely *by* God from place to place within this world - and that he had come into the world.

In the main narrative, the author tells us that Jesus too had come *from* God: *Jesus, knowing that ... <u>he had come from God</u> and was going to God, got up from the table ...* 13:3-4). In verse 8:42, Jesus tells a hostile audience that he had come from and had been sent by God: *"If God were your Father, you would love me, for <u>I came from God</u> and now I am here. I did not come on my own, but <u>he sent me.</u>"* (8:42). Throughout the Gospel Jesus speaks of God as "him who sent me" or as "the one who sent me," and, in his intercessory prayer on behalf of his disciples, Jesus reports to the Father, *"Now they know that everything you have given me is from you; for the words that you gave to me I have given to them, and they*

have received them and know in truth that I came from
you; and they have believed that you sent me." (17:7-8).

To come from God is to come from above. And, not
surprisingly, we find Jesus telling some opponents that he
had come from above: *He said to them, "You are from*
below, I am from above; you are of this world, I am not of
this world." 8:23). It is also not surprising to find Jesus
also saying that he has come down from heaven *("... for I*
have come down from heaven, not to do my own will, but
the will of him who sent me" 6:38).[37] To say that Jesus
had come from God (or from above, or from heaven) is
not to say that his material self (his body) had come from
God. Rather, it is to say that the truth which constituted
Jesus' transcendent self, and which he had embodied, had
come from the transcendent realm.

More obviously relevant to the issue of who *we* are,
are those passages in the Gospel which imply that
otherwise-ordinary people, perhaps people like ourselves
- can come from or be sent by God. One such passage
appears at the end of an argument between Jesus and
some opponents:

> *"... If I tell you the truth, why do you not believe*
> *me? Whoever is from God hears the words of*
> *God. The reason you do not hear them is that you*
> *are not from God."* (8:46-47).

---

[37] Jesus also refers to his having come down from heaven (as the
"bread from heaven") in verses 6:41, 6:49, and 6:57.

Here Jesus' is telling these opponents that they are *not* from God. But implicit in his words is the possibility that others – those who do hear the words of God - *are* from God.

Another passage that suggests that otherwise ordinary people have come from God can be found at the end of John the Baptist's testimony to Jesus. In this testimony, some of the Baptist's disciples report that Jesus has been baptizing people[38] with alarming success:

> *They came to John and said to him, "Rabbi, the one who was with you across the Jordan, to whom you testified, here he is baptizing, and all are going to him." 3:26).*

The Baptist responds by saying that whatever capabilities Jesus might have would have to have come from heaven, and reminds his followers of his subordination to Jesus:

> *John answered, "No one can receive anything except what has been given from heaven. You yourselves are my witnesses that I said, 'I am not the Messiah, but I have been sent ahead of him." 3:27-28).*

---

[38] Apparently the Baptist's disciples were mistaken about Jesus baptizing people himself. As the author of the Gospel explains, *Now when Jesus learned that the Pharisees had heard, "Jesus is making and baptizing more disciples than John" - although it was not Jesus himself but his disciples who baptized - he left Judea and started back to Galilee. (4:1-2).*

Then, in what is represented in the NRSV translation as a comment by the author (but might be a continuation of the Baptist's words) we are told,

> *The one who comes from above is above all; the one who is of the earth belongs to the earth and speaks about earthly things. The one who comes from heaven is above all. He testifies to what he has seen and heard, yet no one accepts his testimony.* (3:31-32).

The important question here is: to whom does "the one" in verses 3:31-32 refer? Does it refer to a particular person, e.g., to Jesus? Or does it refer to "one" in a more general sense?

The Greek wording doesn't help us here. The word translated as "the one" is simply "the." The "one" is to be supplied by the reader. And the larger context suggests that "the one" is to be understood in the general sense. Within this passage, the one "who comes from above" is distinguished from the one "who is of the earth," and the one who is of the earth is clearly meant to be understood in a general sense. The one (anyone) who is of the earth ... speaks about earthly things. Analogously, one (anyone) who comes from heaven ... testifies to what he has seen and heard. Perhaps an even stronger reason to believe that "the one" in verses 3:31-32 does not refer to a specific person is that it clearly applies to both the John the Baptist and to Jesus.

Further evidence that Jesus believed that otherwise ordinary people can have come from and been taught by God can be found in a statement that he makes to some listeners who had been complaining about what he said. Jesus first tells them that they cannot come to him unless they are drawn to him by the Father (*"No one can come to me unless drawn by the Father who sent me ..."* 6:44). He then declares:

> *"It is written in the prophets, 'And <u>they shall all be taught by God.</u>' <u>Everyone who has heard and learned from the Father</u> comes to me. Not that anyone has seen the Father except the one who is from God; he has seen the Father."* (6:45-46).

"The one" in this passage refers to anyone taught by God, to *everyone* who has heard and learned from the Father.

Belonging to the truth

In his arraignment before Pilate, Jesus speaks of people who "belong to the truth": *"... Everyone who belongs to the truth listens to my voice."* (18:37). Inasmuch as the truth *is* God, to belong to the truth is to belong to God. And so it is not surprising to find Jesus speaking of his followers as belonging to God, as we do in this passage:

> *"I have made your name known to those whom you gave me from the world. <u>They were yours,</u>*

140

and you gave them to me ... for the words that you gave to me I have given to them, and they have received them and know in truth that I came from you ... I am asking on their behalf ... on behalf of those whom you gave me, because they are yours. All yours are mine and mine are yours ... " (17:6-10).

As Jesus understood it, those who receive the truth are those who belonged to God and were given by God to Jesus, but nevertheless still belong to God as well as to Jesus.

In the aforementioned verse 3:31, having come from above - a prerequisite to having eternal life - is contrasted to being of and belonging to "the earth" (*The one who comes from above is above all; the one who is of the earth belongs to the earth ...*). But more often the contrast is made to belonging to "the world." In verses 15:19-20, Jesus warns his disciples of the reception that awaits them in this world: *"If you belonged to the world, the world would love you as its own. Because you do not belong to the world, but I have chosen you out of the world - therefore the world hates you ... If they persecuted me they will persecute you ... "* Then later, during his prayer of intercession, Jesus asks God to protect his disciples from "the evil one":

"I have given them [the disciples] *your word, and the world has hated them because they do not*

belong to the world, just as I do not belong to the world. I am not asking you to take them out of the world, but I ask you to protect them from the evil one." (17:14-15).

Jesus also asks that they be sanctified (made holy, purified),

"*They do not belong to the world, just as I do not belong to the world. Sanctify them in the truth; your word is truth. ... And for their sakes, I sanctify myself, so that they also may be sanctified in truth.*" (17:16-19).

To belong to the truth, to belong to God, to be sanctified in the truth, is to embody the values of the truth rather than the values of this world. Those who belong to the truth embody:

- Love, not hate (... "*If God were your father, you would love me ...*" 8:42) and (*"If you belonged to the world, the world would love you as its own. Because you do not belong to the world, but I have chosen you out of the world - therefore the world hates you.*" 15:19),

- Peace, not violence or persecution (*"I have said this to you, so that in me you may have peace. In the world you face persecution. But take courage; I have conquered the world.*" 16:33),

- Forgiveness, not condemnation (*Jesus straightened up and said to her* [the woman caught in adultery], *"Woman, where are they? Has no one condemned you?" She said, "No one, sir." And Jesus said, "Neither do I condemn you. ..."* 8:10-11).

- The truth, not lies (*Jesus said to them, "If God were your Father, you would love me, for I came from God and now I am here. Why do you not understand what I say: It is because you cannot accept my word.* <u>*You are from your father the devil*</u>*, and you choose to do your father's desires. He was a murderer from the beginning and does not stand in the truth.* <u>*When he lies, he speaks according to his own nature, for he is a liar and the father of lies.*</u>*"* 8:42-44),

- Openness, not secrecy (*"And this is the judgment, that the light has come into the world, and people loved darkness rather than light because their deeds were evil. For* <u>*all who do evil hate the light and do not come to the light, so that their deeds may not be exposed. But those who do what is true come to the light, so that it may be clearly seen that their deeds have been done in God.*</u>*"* 3:19-20),

143

- Glory *from* God, rather than from the world (*"I do not accept glory from human beings."* ... *"How can you believe when you accept glory from one another and do not seek the glory that comes from the one who alone is God?"* 5:41-44), and

- Glory *for* God, rather than for oneself (*"Those who speak on their own seek their own glory; but the one who seeks the glory of him who sent him is true, and there is nothing false in him."* 7:18).

Abiding in God

To possess eternal life is to abide in God. But the abiding that Jesus had in mind was a mutual relationship, a relationship in which a person abides in God and, simultaneously, God abides in the person. Or, equivalently, the person abides in the truth, and the truth abides the person.

The notion of "abiding," first appears in the Gospel during a confrontation between Jesus and some opponents about his authority to speak for God. Jesus tells his opponents that he has sought to do the will of God (*"... I seek to do not my own will but the will of him who sent me."* 5:30) and claims that God testifies on his behalf (*"There is another who testifies on my behalf, and I know that his testimony to me is true."* 5:32). Several verses later, Jesus repeats this claim and attributes his opponents' failure to believe him to their not having God's word (the truth) abiding in them:

> *"And the Father who sent me has himself testified on my behalf. You have never heard his voice or seen his form, and <u>you do not have his word abiding in you,</u> because you do not believe him whom he has sent."* (5:37-38).

In this passage, to not believe is to not have the word of God abiding in oneself. By implication, to believe is to have the word of God abiding in oneself - and thus have eternal life.

That God's *word* might abide in a person is perhaps not surprising. But Jesus goes further in suggesting, at the end of his "bread of life discourse," that those who eat his flesh and drink his blood abide in *him*, and *he* in them:

> *So Jesus said to them, "... Those who eat my flesh and drink my blood have eternal life, and I will raise them up on the last day; for my flesh is true flesh and my blood is true drink. <u>Those who eat my flesh and drink my blood abide in me, and I in them.</u>"* (6:53-56).

The "flesh" and "blood" of which Jesus speaks here is the truth which he embodied. And so, what Jesus is really saying in this passage is that those accept the truth - and,

in so doing, come to have eternal life - abide in him, and
he in them.

The idea of a person abiding in Jesus, and Jesus
abiding in the person, is expressed again later in the
Gospel, in a passage in which Jesus speaks of himself
metaphorically as "the true vine."

> "*I am the true vine, and my Father is the*
> *vinegrower. ... Abide in me as I abide in you. Just*
> *as the branch cannot bear fruit by itself unless it*
> *abides in the vine, neither can you unless you*
> *abide in me. I am the vine, you are the branches.*
> *Those who abide in me and I in them bear much*
> *fruit ... Whoever does not abide in me is thrown*
> *away like a branch and withers; such branches*
> *are gathered, thrown into the fire and burned. If*
> *you abide in me, and my words abide in you, ask*
> *for whatever you wish, and it will be done for you.*
> *My Father is glorified by this, that you bear much*
> *fruit and become my disciples.* (15:1-8).

Jesus is the vine, God is the vinegrower, and we are
(meant to be) the branches. As branches must abide in the
vine if they are to bear fruit, we must abide in Jesus if we
are to bear fruit (bring others to eternal life). Toward the
end of this passage Jesus changes the expression from "I
abide in you" to "my words abide in you," but this is
another distinction without a difference. Jesus *is* his
words.

The abiding that is spoken of in John's Gospel is mutual - the truth abides in the person, and the person abides in the truth; the person abides in Jesus, and Jesus abides in the person (*"... Abide in me as I abide in you..."*). If we abide in Jesus and he in us we will be able to ask for whatever we wish (*"... ask for whatever you wish, and it will be done for you..."*). However, there is a catch. The catch is that, if we have the truth abiding in us we will be able to wish for only that which God (the truth) allows. This condition is suggested in a statement that Jesus makes to his disciples after announcing his imminent departure from this world.

> *"Very truly, I tell you, the one who believes in me will also do the works that I do and, in fact, will do greater works than these, because I am going to the Father. I will do whatever you ask in my name, so that the Father may be glorified in the Son. If in my name you ask me for anything, I will do it."* (14:12-13).

To ask in Jesus' name is to ask in accord with his teaching, that is, in accord with the truth to which he testified.

What God/the truth calls us to do is to bring love into being in this, the material world, and for us to serve as his agents in making this happen. Not surprisingly then, in the verses immediately following verses 15:1-8, the focus moves from "my words" to "my love": *"As the Father*

has loved me, so I have loved you; <u>abide in my love</u>. If
you keep my commandments, you will <u>abide in my love</u>,
just as I have kept my Father's commandments and <u>abide</u>
<u>in his love</u>. " (15:9-10).

In anticipation of his death, Jesus attempts to comfort
his disciples by telling them that God will send another
Advocate, "the Spirit of Truth" to be with them in his
place:

> *"If you love me, you will keep my commandments.*
> *And I will ask <u>the Father, and he will give you</u>*
> *<u>another Advocate, to be with you forever</u>. "This is*
> *<u>the Spirit of truth</u>, whom the world cannot receive,*
> *because it neither sees him nor knows him. You*
> *know him, because <u>he abides with you, and he will</u>*
> *<u>be in you</u>. "* (14:15-17).

The Spirit of truth *already* abides with those who love
Jesus and keep his commandments - and this spirit will
remain in them.

To have eternal life is to mutually abide in the
transcendent (in the truth, in God, and in the Spirit of
truth). We might think of a person who has eternal life as
having one foot in this world and the other in the
transcendent.

Being in God

Closely related to the idea of *abiding* in the truth - and perhaps taking it a step further - is the idea of *being* in God. As was the case with abiding, the idea of being *in* God is frequently expressed in a mutual sense: God being in a person and the person being in God. The first instance of this language appears after Jesus has been charged with blasphemy during the Feast of Dedication[39] in Jerusalem. As part of his defense, Jesus makes the following argument:

> *"If I am not doing the works of my Father, then do not believe me. But if I do them, even though you do not believe me, believe the works, so that you may know and understand that the Father is in me and I am in the Father.* (10:37-38).

For Jesus to think of the Father as being in him is interesting by itself. Perhaps Jesus saw the Father as being in him because the word of God was in him. But Jesus also understood himself to be in the Father. What could he have meant by this? His material self, his tangible self, was clearly in this world. In what sense

---

[39] "The Feast of Dedication, today Hannukah, ... was a Jewish festival observed for eight days from the 25th of Kislev (usually in December, but occasionally late November .... It was instituted in the year 165 B.C. by Judas Maccabeus, his brothers, and the elders of the congregation of Israel in commemoration of the reconsecration of the Jewish Temple in Jerusalem." Excerpted from *Wikipedia*, article on "Dedication," August 21, 2014.

then could Jesus have understood himself to be in the
Father? Undoubtedly what Jesus meant was that his
transcendent self (his true self) was in the Father.

Jesus' relationship with the Father can be thought of
as mutual indwelling. Jesus speaks of this relationship
again during what can be thought of as his farewell
address (verses 13:31-16:33). During this address one of
his disciples, Philip, asks Jesus to show them the Father,
and Jesus replies,

> *"Have I been with you all this time, Philip, and
> you still do not know me? Whoever has seen me
> has seen the Father. How can you say, 'Show us
> the Father? Do you not believe that <u>I am in the
> Father, and the Father is in me</u>? The words that I
> say to you I do not speak on my own; but the
> <u>Father who dwells in me</u> does his works. Believe
> me that <u>I am in the Father and the Father is in me</u>
> ... "* (14:9-11)

This passage adds the thought that the indwelling of the
Father in Jesus accounts for the works that Jesus
performs. The Father works in and through Jesus. I am
inclined to think of the Father's works as encompassing
both Jesus' testimony to the truth *and* his audience's
acceptance of his testimony.

The references to "seeing" in the above passage
(*"Whoever has seen me has seen the Father."*) do not

refer to seeing in the literal sense. How do we know this? Because, as the author of the Gospel points out in the prologue, *No one has ever seen God.* (1:18) One does not "see" God in the literal sense, even after having "seen" Jesus in the literal sense. The references to seeing in verses 14:9-11 refer to coming to understand, and recognize as true, what Jesus was saying. To have "seen" Jesus in this sense *is* to have "seen" the Father.

Jesus' notion of "being in" the Father is then extended to encompass not only himself but his disciples as well:

> *"In a little while the world will no longer see me, but you will see me; because I live, you also will live. On that day you will know that I am in my Father, and you in me, and I in you."* (14:19-20).

The true disciple is in Jesus, and Jesus is in the true disciple - and both are in the Father. That Jesus also understood the Father to be in him is made explicit later, in his prayer for intercession on behalf of the disciples, and on behalf of all who will come to believe:

> *"I ask not only on behalf of these, but also on behalf of those who will believe in me through their word, that they may all be one. As you, Father, are in me and I am in you, may they also be in us, so that the world may believe that you sent me."* (17:20-21).

As the Father is in Jesus and Jesus is in the Father, "those who will believe" will be in both Jesus and the Father. The point appears to be that one's true self - the self that comes into being in response to the truth - has its locus of being not in this world, but in the transcendent. The mutual being in God applies to all those who have come to have eternal life.

Although it might seem a small matter, having already accepted that one can *be* in God and God can be in oneself, Jesus understood that a person can also *act* (do) in God. This can be seen in what Jesus says at the end of his conversation with Nicodemus:

> *"... all who do evil hate the light and do not come to the light, so that their deeds may not be exposed. But <u>those who do what is true</u> come to the light, so that it may be clearly seen that <u>their deeds have been done in God</u>."* (3:20-21).

In what sense might the deeds of "those who do what is true" be done in God? Of course, their deeds might be done in accord with the will of God. But this passage is saying more. Those who do what is true are acting while *in* God, while being simultaneously in this world and in the transcendent.

Being one with God

Eternal life is also associated in the Gospel with
"oneness" with God. In the continuation of his prayer of
intercession, Jesus expresses his desire that his followers
might all become "one." He then elaborates on this idea,
and within this elaboration he moves back and forth
between the idea of being *in* God and the idea of being
one with God:

> *"I ask not only on behalf of these* [Jesus' then
> living disciples]*, but also on behalf of those who
> will believe in me through their word, <u>that they
> may all be one.</u> ... "* (17:20-21),

> *"The glory that you have given me I have given
> them, <u>so that they may be one, as we are one.</u>"*
> (17:22), and

> *"<u>I in them and you in me, that they may be
> completely one</u>, so that the world may know that
> you have sent me and have loved them even as you
> have loved me."* (17:23).

In this sequence of verses, Jesus speaks of the possibility
of believers all being one (... *that they all may be one)*,
but perhaps in a "oneness" among themselves, apart from
God and himself. Then, apparently to explain what
oneness might entail, Jesus speaks of the Father being in
him, his being in the Father, and the believers being in

them both (*As you, Father, <u>are in me and I am in you,
may they also be in us</u>*). Next, Jesus speaks of the
believers being one *as* (in the same manner that) he and
God are one (*"... <u>so that they may be one, as we are
one</u>"*). Finally, Jesus links his being *in* the believer, and
God's being *in* him, to the possibility of the believers
being "completely one" with himself and with God (*"... <u>I
in them and you in me, that they may be completely one.
...</u>"*). Inasmuch as Jesus is in us and God is in Jesus, then
God is in us, and we *are* completely one - completely one
with God and with Jesus and with all believers, with all
those who come to have eternal life.

Once we recognize that oneness with God is a state of
being to which all believers can rise, it is not surprising to
find Jesus declaring, in verse 10:30, *"The Father and I
are one."* In the absence of an understanding of oneness
with God and it's applicability to *all* believers, a person
might read Jesus' statement in verse 10:30 as expressing a
unique relationship between Jesus and God. Some have
seen verse 10:30 as having "christological" significance,
i.e., as saying something about the sense in which Jesus is
the "Christ" (or, equivalently, the"Messiah," one anointed
to advance God's purpose in this world). And it does, but
not with the uniqueness that might be read into it.
"Christness" or "Messiahship," is a role to which each
believer is called to fill by the truth. Some have also read
verse 10:30 as indicating that Jesus was, or had claimed to
be, God. But Jesus was not and did not claim to be God.
Verse 10:30 should be read in the context of the Gospel as
a whole. Throughout the Gospel, Jesus is careful to

distinguish between himself and God (*"... I have not spoken on my own, but the Father who sent me has himself given me a commandment about what to say and what to speak."* (12:49). And he recognized his subordination to God (*"... the Father is greater than I"* (14:28). What Jesus meant in verse 10:30 is that he was one *with* God, as he anticipates the believer will be also.

Knowing God

The most direct statement of what eternal life is appears relatively late in the Gospel of John, when Jesus tells the Father: *"And <u>this is eternal life that they may know you, the only true God,</u> and Jesus Christ whom you have sent."* (17:3). To have eternal life is to know God. Perhaps, rather than thinking of eternal life as the *same thing* as knowing God, it would be best to think of Jesus' words as meaning that in coming to have eternal life one comes to know God.

I am inclined to think that the "knowing" to which Jesus refers in verse 17:3 goes beyond knowing God in the cognitive sense and includes knowing God experientially, that is as a result of having lived one's life in accord with the truth. This experiential knowing is indicated in Jesus' conversation with some of his followers who no longer believed in him. Jesus tells them, *"If you continue in my word, you are truly my disciples; and <u>you will know the truth, and the truth will make you free.</u>"* (8:31-32). To continue in Jesus' word is to live one's life in accord with the truth to which he testified. What is involved in living in accord with the truth will be addressed in Part III (What We Are Meant to Be Doing).

Living eternally in God

The expression, "eternal life," first appears in the Gospel of John in Jesus' conversation with Nicodemus. Jesus has just explained his role (as the Son of Man) with reference to Moses: *"And just as Moses lifted up the serpent in the wilderness, so must the Son of Man be lifted up, that whoever believes in him may have eternal life."* (3:14-15).[40] Verses 3:14 and 15 do not tell us much about eternal life, but the next verse does: *"For God so loved the world that he gave his only Son, so that everyone who believes in him may not perish but may have eternal life."* (3:16). Not perishing is spoken of again in connection with eternal life later in the Gospel when, during a religious festival in Jerusalem, Jesus is pressured to declare that he is the Messiah (*So the Jews gathered around him and said to him, "How long will you keep us in suspense? If you are the Messiah, tell us plainly."*(10:24). Jesus responds by telling them that he has already told them, but they have not believed. He then adds, *"My sheep hear my voice. I know them and*

---

[40] As the author later explains (*"And I, when I am lifted up from the earth, will draw all people to myself." He said this to indicate the kind of death he was to die.* 12:32-33), the phrase "lifted up" refers to Jesus' being lifted up upon the cross at his crucifixion.

they follow me. I give them eternal life, and they will never perish." (10:27-28). Hearing Jesus' "voice" (comprehending and recognizing the truth of what Jesus is saying) and following him (following his teaching and example) leads to eternal life - and not perishing.

Jesus also tells his listeners that those who eat the bread that he represents (those who accept his teaching) will not die; but rather will "live forever":

> *"I am the bread of life. ... This is the bread that comes down from heaven, so that one may eat of it and not die. I am the living bread that came down from heaven. Whoever eats of this bread will live forever ...* 6:48-51).

In this passage, Jesus first identifies himself as "the bread of life," and then as "the living bread." Those who "eat" of this bread - those who take in and digest the truth - will not die, but will live forever. And as we have already seen, Jesus tells Martha (a sister of Lazarus) that those who believe in him will never die (*Jesus said to her, "... Those who believe in me, even though they die, will live, and everyone who lives and believes in me will never die."* 11:25-26).

All of these expressions - not or never perishing, not or never dying, and living forever - indicate that eternal life brings with it immortality. But immortality in what sense? The immortality that Jesus had in mind is best

157

revealed in his conversation with Martha. One's material self will inevitably die a natural death. The immortality that Jesus' words offer is immortality of the transcendent self. It is not the continuation, or resumption and continuation, of material existence for all time. Rather, it is immortality of the self that has been brought into being by the truth, the transcendent self, the self that abides eternally in God.

The various attributes associated with eternal life account for our ability to play a meaningful role in realizing the purpose behind existence. Inasmuch as we belong to God, we are drawn to the truth, we listen for it, and adopt its values as our own. Inasmuch as we have come from above, we have been taught by God, we have heard and learned from the Father. We are thus able to recognize the truth when we hear it (for more on this, see Chapter 8: Believing). Inasmuch as we have been sent by God we recognize our responsibility to testify to the truth. Inasmuch as we abide in God, and he in us, we maintain a continuing relationship with God.

The attributes of those who have eternal life apply to Jesus, as he is represented in the Gospel of John. But Jesus is also spoken of as "the Son of Man" and "the Son of God." What do these terms mean? And to whom do they apply? These questions will be addressed in the next chapter.

Eternal Life

Points to Keep in Mind

- To have eternal life is to have been born of God, born from above.

- To have eternal life is to belong to the truth; to be drawn to, and embody the values of, the truth.

- To have eternal life is to abide mutually *in* God - God *in* oneself, oneself in God.

- To have eternal life is to know, and be one with, God.

- To have eternal life is to be immortal, to live eternally in God.

Chapter 7

SON OF MAN/SON OF GOD

"No one has ascended into heaven except the one who descended from heaven, the Son of Man. And just as Moses lifted up the serpent in the wilderness, so must the Son of Man be lifted up, that whoever believes in him may have eternal life. " (3:13-15)

In the Gospel of John, Jesus often speaks of "the Son of Man." This expression is used only by Jesus except for in one instance, when a crowd asks him what he means by it. In this instance Jesus tells the crowd, *"The hour has come for the Son of Man to be glorified. Very truly, I tell you, unless a grain of wheat falls to the earth and dies, it remains just a single grain; but if it dies, it bears much fruit. "* (12:23-24). Jesus then speaks of being "lifted up from the earth" (*"And I, when I am lifted up from the earth, will draw all people to myself. "* 12:32). The author of the Gospel then tells us, *He said this to indicate the kind of death he was to die.* (12:33). At this point, the crowd complains to Jesus, *"We have heard from the law that the Messiah remains forever. How can you say that the Son of Man must be lifted up? Who is this Son of Man? "* (12:34).

The people listening to Jesus were not familiar with the expression, "the Son of Man," and they did not know to whom it referred. The crowd was clearly skeptical about Jesus' claims. Even the man who had been blind from birth, and whose eyes had been opened by Jesus, was still unfamiliar with the expression. When Jesus asks him, *"Do you believe in the Son of Man?"* (9:35), the man answers, *"And who is he, sir? Tell me, so that I may believe in him."* (9:36). Jesus then tells him, *"You have seen him, and the one speaking with you is he."* (9:37).

The expression, the Son of Man, was problematic for Jesus' listeners in his day, and it remains problematic for us today. To whom the expression refers, and what Jesus meant by it, are matters of continuing debate among scholars and theologians.[41] Nevertheless, by examining the evidence within the Gospel of John, it *is* possible to determine what Jesus meant. In this chapter, we will do just that, with particular attention to what Jesus' testimony about "the Son of Man" tells us about who *we* are - or rather, who we *could* be.

Determining what Jesus meant by "the Son of Man" is complicated somewhat by the fact that, in the Gospel, Jesus also speaks of "the Son" and "the Son of God." Conveniently, for our purpose all three expressions refer

---

[41] See *The Son of Man Debate: A History and Evaluation* by Delbert Burkett, Cambridge University Press, 1999; "The Martyrdom of the Son of Man" by Theodore W. Jennings, Jr., in *Text and Logos: The Humanistic Interpretation of the New Testament,* Scholars Press, Atlanta Georgia, 1990; *The Origin of Christology* by C.F.D. Moule, Cambridge University Press, 1977; and, more recently, *'Who is This Son of Man?': The Latest Scholarship on a Puzzling Expression of the Historical Jesus,* Hurtado, Larry W., and Paul L Owens, eds., T&T Clark, New York, 2011.

to the same person. This simplifies the task of determining what Jesus meant because we can use everything that is said about each Son to determine what he meant by the Son of Man. That all three expressions refer to the same person can be seen in a passage in which Jesus discusses the effect of the Son's voice on "the dead":

> *"Very truly, I tell you, the hour is coming, and is now here, when the dead will hear the voice of <u>the Son of God</u>, and those who hear will live. For just as the Father has life in himself, so has he granted <u>the Son</u> also to have life in himself; and he has given him authority to execute judgment, because he is <u>the Son of Man</u>." (5:25-27)*

Here, all three expressions appear in the same brief passage, and that the Son *is* the Son of Man is stated explicitly at the end of the passage ("he is the Son of Man"). That the Son of God is also the Son is implied by the linkage between the sentences ("For ...").

The equivalence and interchangeability of the three "Son" expressions is also evident in Jesus' explanation, to Nicodemus, of his role in saving the world:

> *"No one has ascended into heaven except the one who descended from heaven, the Son of Man. And just as Moses lifted up the serpent in the wilderness, so must <u>the Son of Man</u> be lifted up, that whoever believes in him may have eternal life. For God so loved the world that he gave his only*

> *Son ... "Indeed, God did not send <u>the Son</u> into the
> world to condemn the world, but in order that the
> world might be saved through him. Those who
> believe in him are not condemned; but those who
> do not believe are condemned already, because
> they have not believed in the name of <u>the only Son
> of God</u>.* (3:13-18)

Here again, the linkages between the sentences ("For,"
"Indeed," and "him" used in reference to the Son) indicate
that the Son of Man *is* the Son *is* the Son of God.

Why did Jesus (or the author of the Gospel) use three
different expressions in referring to the Son of Man? I am
inclined to think that he did so in order to establish
control over the meaning of each. For Jesus, the
controlling expression is "the Son of Man." This
expression originates with him; no one else in the Gospel
uses it except to ask what it means; no one evidences any
recognition or understanding of it; and Jesus uses "the
Son of Man" more often (11 times) than he does "the Son
of God" (perhaps 4 times). By introducing and defining
the Son of Man, Jesus is thereby redefining what it means
to be the Son of God. The Son of God is a person who
does what the Son of Man does. What *Jesus*, as the Son
of Man, did was to testify to the truth, to make of his life
and death a testament to the truth. Thus, inasmuch as
Jesus was the Son of Man, the Son of God is a person
who testifies to the truth, who makes of his (or her) life a
testament to the truth.

But I have gotten ahead of myself. We have yet to fully establish who the Son of Man is.

The Son of Man as Jesus

When Jesus spoke of the Son of Man, to whom was he referring? The evidence shows that Jesus used the expression to refer to himself. This is clear in verse 8:28, when he tells an uncomprehending audience, *"When you have lifted up the Son of Man, then you will realize that I am he ...."* He was also referring to himself in the aforementioned verse 9:37. But even without this direct evidence we would be able to recognize Jesus as the Son of Man because of the many parallels between (a) what the Gospel says about Jesus and (b) what it says about the Son of Man (or, simply, the Son):

- Jesus came down from heaven (*"I am the living bread that came down from heaven. ..."* 6:51). The Son of Man came down from heaven (*"No one has ascended into heaven except the one who descended from heaven, the Son of Man."* 3:13).

- Jesus will ascend to God (*Jesus said to her, "Do not hold on to me, for I have not yet ascended to the Father. But go to my brothers and say to them, "I am ascending to my Father and your Father, to my God and Your God."* 20:17). The Son of Man will ascend (or might be seen to be ascending) to where he was before (*But Jesus ...*

165

said to them, "Does it offend you? Then what if you were to see the Son of Man ascending to where he was before?" 6:61-62).

- Jesus was sent by God (*Jesus said to them, "... I came from God and now I am here. I did not come on my own, but he sent me."* 8:42), see also 6:57. The Son was sent by the Father (*"... Anyone who does not honor the Son does not honor the Father who sent him."* 5:23).

- Jesus came to save the world (*"I do not judge anyone who hears my words and does not keep them, for I came not to judge the world but to save the world."* 12:47). The Son was sent to save the world (*"Indeed, God did not send the Son into the world to condemn the world, but in order that the world might be saved through him."* 3:17).

- Jesus could do nothing on his own (**"I can do nothing on my own. ..."* 5:30). The Son can do nothing on his own (*Jesus said to them, "Very truly, I tell you, the Son can do nothing on his own, but only what he sees the Father doing ..."*5:19).

- The Father showed Jesus what he was doing (*"I declare what I have seen in the Father's presence ..."* 8:38). The Father shows the Son what he is doing (*"The Father loves the Son and shows him all that he himself is doing ..."* 5:20).

- Jesus testifies to the truth (*"For this I was born, and for this I came into the world, to testify to the truth."* 18:37). The Son gives "the food that endures" (*"Do not work for the food that perishes, but for the food that endures for eternal life, which the Son of Man will give you. For it is on him that God the Father has set his seal."* 6:27).

- Jesus made God known (*"Righteous Father, the world does not know you, but I know you; and these know you that you have sent me. I made your name known to them ..."* (17:25-26). The Son made God known (*No one has ever seen God. It is the only Son,*[42] *who is close to the Father's heart, who has made him known.*1:18).

- Jesus was to be "lifted up" (put to death upon the cross) (*"And I, when I am lifted up from the earth, will draw all people to myself."* 12:32). The Son of Man must be lifted up (*And just as Moses lifted up the serpent in the wilderness, so must the Son of Man be lifted up ..."* 3:14).

Jesus clearly thought of himself as "the Son of Man." But why did he choose to refer to himself in the third person in this way? It would be understandable if Jesus'

---

[42] See footnote 3.

listeners had been familiar with the expression and had
expectations concerning the Son of Man - and if Jesus
wanted to represent himself as the person who had come
to fulfill these expectations. But Jesus' audience was not
familiar with the expression and therefore could not have
had expectations concerning a Son of Man. So, why did
he introduce the expression, and refer to himself as, the
Son of Man?

Perhaps Jesus' purpose in speaking of the Son of Man
was not just to tell us who *he* was, but to, at the same
time, tell us about who *we* are - or rather who we are
meant to be. I believe - and the evidence in the Gospel
will show - that Jesus understood, and meant *us* to
understand, the expression, "the Son of Man," in a
corporate sense, that is, as referring to a category of
being, a category of being that could and would include
others in addition to himself.

The Corporate Son of Man

The evidence in the Gospel that supports a corporate
understanding of "the Son of Man" includes: (a) the
anonymity of most of the Son of Man sayings, (b) the
passages that speak of "children of God" and of God as
Father, and (c) the parallels between what is said of the
Son of Man and what is said of the believer. We will look
at this evidence, draw tentative conclusions, and then will
address the "problem passages," passages in the Gospel

that contain evidence to the contrary, passages that should be recognized and accounted for.

Anonymity

While all of the Son of Man (and Son, and Son of God) sayings apply to Jesus, in only two (verses 8:28 and 9:37) does Jesus directly refer to himself as the Son of Man. But even while referring to himself as the Son of Man, Jesus could have been thinking of "the Son of Man" as a category of being in relation to God (to the truth), and of himself as an instance of "Sonship," the instance that defines the category.

In the other sayings, Jesus reveals himself as the Son of Man only indirectly, as he does in this passage:

> *So Jesus said to them, "Very truly, I tell you unless you eat the flesh of the Son of Man and drink his blood, you have no life in you. Those who eat my flesh and drink my blood have eternal life, and I will raise them up on the last day."* (6:53-54).

Jesus could have said the same thing if he had thought that there were, or would be, other Sons of Man, other Sons who would provide *their* "flesh" and "blood" (the truth). At the very least, applicability of a passage to Jesus is not evidence of its non-applicability to others.

In most of the Son of Man passages there is no clear indication who the Son of Man is. These "anonymous" Son of Man passages include:

> *And he [Jesus] said to him, "Very truly I tell you, you will see heaven opened and the angels of God ascending and descending on <u>the Son of Man</u>."* (1:51),

> *"No one has ascended into heaven except <u>the one who descended from heaven, the Son of Man</u>."* (3:13)

> *"Very truly, I tell you, the hour is coming and is now here, when the dead will hear the voice of the Son of God, and those who hear will live. For just as the Father has life in himself, so he has granted the Son also to have life in himself; and he has given him authority to execute judgment, because he is <u>the Son of Man</u>. Do not be astonished at this; for the hour is coming when all who are in their graves will hear his voice."* (5:25-28), and

> *"Do not work for the food that perishes, but for the food that endures for eternal life, which <u>the Son of Man</u> will give you. For it is on him that God the Father has set his seal."* (6:27).

The passages in which Jesus speaks of the Son of Man tell us about: (a) The Son's origin (his descent from heaven), (b) his role in advancing God's purpose (providing "the food that endures for eternal life," i.e. the truth), and (c) the basis for his authority (having received the truth from God, having been granted life in himself, and having received God's seal).

The Son of Man passages are not unlike the passages that speak of "the one who," such as:

The one who comes from above is above all; the one who is of the earth belongs to the earth and speaks about earthly things. The one who comes from heaven is above all. He testifies to what he has seen and heard, yet no one accepts his testimony. (3:31-32),

"... the one who seeks the glory of him who sent him is true, and there is nothing false in him." (7:18),

"The one who enters by the gate is the shepherd of the sheep. The gatekeeper opens the gate for him, and the sheep hear his voice." (10:2), and

"Very truly, I tell you, the one who believes in me will also do the works that I do and, in fact, will do greater works than these ..." (14:12).

As in the Son of Man passages, "the one who" passages speak of an unnamed individual, or category of individual. As in the Son of Man passages, "the one who" is described in terms of his (or her) origin, role and authority. In verse 14:12 it is obvious that Jesus thought of "the one who" as being someone other than himself.

Children of God/God as Father

The Gospel of John speaks of people being enabled to become children of God, being born of God, and having God as their Father. Already in the prologue the author of the Gospel tells us that Jesus empowered people to become children of God, and the author refers to these people as having been born of God: *But to all who received him, who believed in his name, he gave power to become children of God, who were born ... of God.*(1:12). The "all" in this verse and the plural "children" make it clear that the author of the Gospel envisioned the possibility of more than one child of God. But who would these people be? As verse 1:12 puts it, they are those who "receive Jesus" (accept the truth that he represented) and "believe in his name" (believe as he taught). They are empowered by the truth to become children, Sons (or Daughters) of God - and thus Sons of Man.

Throughout the Gospel of John, Jesus refers to God as "Father." The vast majority of these references are to "*the* Father" (80 times in 65 verses) and "*my* Father" (20 times in 19 verses). The question before us is whether Jesus thought of God as the Father of others in addition to himself. Indirect evidence that he did appears in Jesus' argument with some opponents about their relationship with the Father. When the opponents argue, *"We are not illegitimate children; we have one father, God himself."* Jesus tells them, *"If God were your Father, you would love me, for I came from God and now am here."* (8:41-

42). Here Jesus speaks of God as being others' Father as if it were a possibility. More direct, and conclusive, evidence that Jesus thought of God as the Father of others as well as himself appears late in the Gospel when, after his death, Jesus appears to Mary and tells her, *"Do not hold onto me, because I have not yet ascended to the Father. But go to my brothers and say to them, 'I am ascending to my Father and your Father, to my God and your God."* (20:17).[43] Jesus understood God as being the Father of his disciples, that is, of those who followed his teaching. Perhaps this is why Jesus refers to "*the* Father" more often than to "*my* Father." In any case, inasmuch as God is a person's Father, the person can be thought of as a Son or Daughter of God and Man.

Parallels

Additional support for the idea that the Son of Man is a category of being that encompasses others in addition to Jesus, can be found in the parallels between what is said of the Son of Man and what is said of others. These parallels include:

- The Son of Man has descended from heaven: *"No one has ascended into heaven except the one who descended from heaven, the Son of Man."* (3:13); others can be born from above, or can have come

---

[43] That Jesus thought of God as the Father of others in addition to himself is manifestly obvious in what is commonly referred to as the Lord's Prayer. The version of the prayer in the Gospel of Matthew (Matthew 6:9-13) opens with Jesus saying, "Our Father who art in heaven …" (Matt: 6:9-13).

from God: *"Very truly, I tell you, no one can see the kingdom of God without being born from above."*(3:3), *"Do not be astonished that I said to you, 'You must be born from above.'"* (3:7), and *"Whoever is from God hears the words of God. ..."* (8:47).

- The Son was sent by God: *"For God so loved the world that he gave his only Son ... Indeed, God did not send the Son into the world to condemn the world, but in order that the world might be saved through him."* (3:16-17); Others have been sent: *There was a man sent from God, whose name was John.* (1:6), and *Jesus answered, "... We must work the works of him who sent [us][44] while it is day ...* (9:3-4).

- The Son is taught by God: *Jesus said to them, "Very truly, I tell you, the Son can do nothing on his own, but only what he sees the Father doing; ... The Father loves the Son and shows him all that he himself is doing ..."* (5:19-20). Anonymous others also have been, and will be, taught by God: *"It is written in the prophets, 'And they shall all be taught by God,' Everyone who has heard and learned from the Father comes to*

---

[44] I have changed the "me" of the NRSV translation to "us" in verse 9.4 because it is more consistent with the larger context in the Gospel of John, and because the earliest witnesses (ancient manuscripts of the Gospel) read "us," rather than "me."

Son of Man/Son of God

me." (6:45), and *"Whoever is from God hears the words of God. ..."* (8:47).

-   The Son of Man testifies to the truth: *"Do not work for the food that perishes, but for the food* [the Word or truth] *that endures for eternal life, which the Son of Man will give you. ..."* (6:27). John the Baptist testified, and anonymous others will testify, to the truth: *"You sent messengers to John, and he testified to the truth."* (5:33), *The one who comes from heaven is above all. ... He testifies to what he has seen and heard...* (3:31-32), and *"He whom God has sent speaks the words of God, for he gives the Spirit without measure."* (3:34).

-   The Son of Man must be killed: *"And just as Moses lifted up the serpent in the wilderness, so must the Son of Man be lifted up* [crucified] *..."* (3:14) and *Jesus answered them, "The hour has come for the Son of Man to be glorified. Very truly, I tell you, unless a grain of wheat falls into the earth and dies, it remains a single grain; but if it dies, it bears much fruit."* (12:23-24); others too will be killed: *"They will put you* [Jesus' followers] *out of the synagogues. Indeed, an hour is coming when those who kill you will think that by doing so they are offering worship to God."* (16:2)

Interim conclusion

Evidence throughout the Gospel suggests and supports the conclusion that Jesus used the expression, "the Son of Man," to refer to a person (any person) who believes and lives in accord with the truth.

Problem passages

The only serious "problem passages" in the Gospel - passages that directly contradict the corporate understanding of the Son of Man (and of the Son of God) - are those that refer to an *only* Son.   Three verses in the Gospel of John do so, and they are:

No one has ever seen God. It is the only Son, who is close to the Father's heart, who has made him known. (1:18),

"For God so loved the world that he gave his only Son, so that everyone who believes in him may not perish but may have eternal life." (3:16), and

"Those who believe in him are not condemned; but those who do not believe are condemned already, because they have not believed in the name of the only Son of God." (3:18).

The first of these three verses (verse 1:18) comes at the end of the prologue. It was written by the author (or by a final editor) of the Gospel after Jesus' death, and it may or may not reflect Jesus' own understanding. What the verse does establish is that the author (or final editor) wanted the reader to think of Jesus as God's only Son. Verses 3:16 and 3:18 may or may not be attributed to Jesus. As was pointed out earlier (see footnote in Chapter 5) Jesus' speech may end with verse 3:15, or it may continue on to include verses 3:16 and 3:18. In the many verses in John's Gospel that are clearly attributed to Jesus, and that mention a Son, the word "only" is nowhere to be found. In short, there is no clear evidence in the Gospel of John that Jesus thought of himself as being an *only* Son - whether of God or of Man.

Another reason to discount (or benignly ignore) the uniqueness claims regarding the Sonship of Jesus is that nothing in his testimony to the truth, and nothing in our reception of the truth, depends on Jesus being, or being thought of as, an *only* Son. All that our beneficial reception of the truth depends on is (a) that the truth to which Jesus testified is true and *the* truth behind existence and (b), if it is true, that we come to understand and recognize it as such. The truth working within us will take care of everything else.

A third, and more substantive, reason to ignore the uniqueness claims is that, according to the Gospel, all who those come to embody the truth abide in Jesus, and he in them. They are one with Jesus, and Jesus is one with them. Moreover, Jesus and the believer are of the same substance (the truth). In short, the believer and Jesus are essentially the same person. And so, claims of an "only Son" don't make sense unless the only Son is itself understood in an inclusive rather than exclusive sense.

The conclusion that best fits all of the evidence in the text of the Gospel is that Jesus understood - and meant *us* to understand - the expression, "the Son of Man," in a corporate sense, to refer to a new category of being in relation to God.[45] From this perspective, Jesus can be thought of as *a* Son of Man - and *the* Son of Man in that his life is the model for "Sonship."

---

[45] The "corporate" meaning of "the Son of Man" has been recognized by prominent theologians for some time. T.W. Manson has concluded, "When we come to study the use of the term Son of Man in the sayings of Jesus, we should be prepared to find that it may stand for a community comparable to 'the people of the saints of the Most High,' in Dan. vii., and that sometimes this community may be thought of as an aggregate of individuals, at other times as a single corporate entity. Again, we should be prepared to find that this corporate entity is embodied par excellence in Jesus himself, in such a way that his followers, who together with him constitute the Son of Man as a group, may be thought of as extensions of his personality, or as St. Paul puts it later on, limbs of his body. And I think that all the authentic instances of the use of the term 'Son of Man' in the Synoptic Gospels should be interpreted along these lines." ("The Son of Man in Daniel, Enoch and the Gospels," *Bulletin of the John Rylands University Library of Manchester*, 32: 1950. See also, C.D.F. Moule ("... I conclude that 'the Son of Man,' so far from being a title evolved from current apocalyptic thought by the early Church and put by it onto the lips of Jesus, is among the most important symbols used by Jesus himself to describe his vocation and that of those whom he summoned to be with him."), *The Origin of Christology*, Cambridge: Cambridge University Press, 1977, p. 22.

Blasphemy?

Is it a stretch to think of a human as a Son of Man and Son of God? Was it for Jesus? What does the Gospel suggest? After Jesus makes his seemingly outrageous statement, *"The Father and I are one"* (10:30), his fellow Jews take up stones to kill him (10:31), and Jesus asks, *"I have shown you many good works from the Father. For which of these are you going to stone me?"* (10:32) His opponents answer, *"It is not for a good work that we are going to stone you, but for blasphemy, because you, though only a human being, are making yourself God."* (10:33) And Jesus offers his defense:

> *"Is it not written in your law, 'I said, you are gods'? If those to whom the word of God came were called 'gods' - and the scripture cannot be annulled - can you say that the one whom the Father has sanctified and sent into the world is blaspheming because I said, 'I am God's Son'?"* (10:34-36)

In this defense against the charge of blasphemy, Jesus refers to what appears to be a stronger claim of godliness embedded in scripture (Psalm 82). He tells his accusers that "those to whom the word of God came were called "gods"[46] and reminds them that "scripture cannot be

---

[46] In Psalm 82, the "gods" are not said to be "those to whom the word of God came," but rather (see verse 82:8) "children of the Most High," the Most High in this case being God. The wording of the psalm provides an even better justification for thinking of Jesus as the

annulled." He concludes by asking his accusers if they can (legitimately) say "the one whom the Father has sanctified and sent into the world" is blaspheming when he said, 'I am God's Son'?" In this defense, Jesus switches the focus from "the one whom the Father has sanctified and sent" to himself. This is understandable because Jesus saw himself as one whom the Father had sanctified and sent. However, later in the Gospel, he recognized the possibility of others also being sanctified and sent:

> *"They* [Jesus' disciples] *do not belong to the world, just as I do not belong to the world. Sanctify them in the truth; your word is truth. As you have sent me into the world, so I have sent them into the world. And for their sakes I sanctify myself, so that they also may be sanctified in truth.* (17:16-19)

In this passage, Jesus speaks of sending the disciples into the world himself, but Jesus can do nothing on his own. It will be the Father (the truth) sending the disciples into the world, the Father working through Jesus and in the disciples. And just as Jesus was justified in saying, "I am God's Son," so will his disciples be justified. They too will be Sons of God, Sons of Man.

In addressing how best to understand and express the relationship between Jesus and God, a majority of the

---

Son of God (and for those to whom the word of God comes as Sons of God and Sons of Man).

bishops at the First council at Nicea in 325 CE approved the wording of a creed (the Nicene Creed) which asserts that Jesus was "of the same substance" as the Father. In the context of the Gospel of John, that substance would be the truth. Jesus, like the Father, was constituted by the truth. Similarly, all "to whom the word of God comes," all who believe and bring their lives into accord with the truth, are of the same substance as the Father. Not gods (those to whom the word of God came), not God, but of the same *substance* as God.

In Part II (Chapters 5-7) we have addressed the question, Who are we?, as this topic is treated in the Gospel of John. In Part III (Chapters 8-10) we will look at what the Gospel (Jesus' testimony in the Gospel) tells us about what a person would need to do in order to have eternal life, and participate in realizing the purpose behind existence. We will begin (in Chapter 8) by looking at the need to believe, with emphasis on *what* we are to believe, and on the basis for believing.

Points to Keep in Mind

- **In his testimony to the truth, Jesus used the expression, "the Son of Man," in a corporate sense, to refer to a category of being in relation to God, a category which encompasses all who have come to believe, and to live their lives in accord with, the truth.**

- **Inasmuch as the Son of Man is defined without reference to gender, we should understand the expression, Son of Man (and of God), as encompassing both Sons and Daughters.**

- **In introducing the category, the Son of Man, Jesus was at the same time redefining what it meant to be a Son of God. The Son of Man *is* the Son of God.**

Chapter 8

BELIEVING

"Do not work for the food that perishes, but for the food that endures for eternal life, which the Son of Man will give you. For it is on him that God the Father has set his seal. Then they said to him, "What must we do to do the works of God?" Jesus answered them, "This is the work of God, that you believe in him whom he has sent." (6:27-29)

What must a person do in order to have eternal life and participate in realizing the purpose behind existence? According to the Gospel of John, he or she must do just three things: believe the truth, love one another, and testify to the truth. In this chapter we will establish what the Gospel tells us about the need to believe - with emphasis on *what* we are to believe and *how* we are able to know the truth. The need to love and to testify will be addressed in Chapters 9 and 10.

Believing, in the Gospel

The word "believe" - or a variant thereof - appears approximately one-hundred times in the Gospel of John. In most of the passages in which it appears, believing is associated with having eternal life or with serving as an agent of God (of the truth).

Believing

In the prologue of the Gospel, believing is associated with becoming "children of God" (an attribute of eternal life). This is how the author of the Gospel put it: *But to all who received him, who believed in his [Jesus'] name, he gave power to become children of God ...* (1:12). Those who were empowered to become children of God are those who "believed in his name." But what did the author mean by the expression "believe in his name"? In Jesus' lifetime - and during the time in which the Gospel was being written - to "believe in a person's name" meant to believe as that person taught[47]. And so verse 1:12 is telling us that all who believed Jesus' teaching, his testimony to the truth, were (presumably thereby) empowered to become children of God.

While the prologue of the Gospel of John speaks of belief as the key to becoming a child of God, the main narrative more often speaks of belief as the key to eternal life. The link between believing and eternal life is first made at the end of (or perhaps immediately following) Jesus' conversation with Nicodemus: "*For God so loved the world that he gave his only Son, so that everyone who believes in him may not perish but may have eternal life.*" (3:16). Later in the Gospel Jesus makes the point that

---

[47] "First, there is the rabbinic idiom, 'in the name of' ... used to identify from whom teachings originate." *The Didache: Its Jewish Sources and Its Place in Early Judaism and Christianity,* by van de Sandt, Huub, and David Flusser. Assen: Van Gorcum; Minneapolis: Fortress 2002.

anyone who believes already has eternal life: *"Very truly, I tell you, whoever <u>believes</u> has eternal life."* (6:47).

The need to believe is expressed in a variety of ways in the Gospel of John. As we have already seen, verse 1:12 calls for belief "in Jesus' name," verse 3:16 calls for belief "in the Son," and verse 6:47 calls simply for belief without specifying an object of belief. Others passages in the Gospel speak of the need to believe:

- "Jesus" (*"Which of you convicts me of sin? If I tell the truth, why do you not <u>believe me</u>?"* 8:46),

- "in God" (*"Do not let your hearts be troubled. <u>Believe in God</u>, believe also in me."* 14:1),

-
- "in Jesus" (*"Do not let your hearts be troubled. Believe in God, <u>believe also in me</u>."* 14:1),

- "in the light" (*"While you have the light, <u>believe in the light</u>, so that you may become children of light."* 12:36), and

- "specific teachings" (*Jesus said to her, "I am the resurrection and the life. <u>Those who believe in me, even though they die, will live, and everyone who lives and believes in me will never die</u>. Do you believe this?"* 11:25-26).

At the core of each of these expressions is the need to believe Jesus, specifically to believe the truth to which Jesus testified.

- To believe "in Jesus' name" (as he taught) and to believe specific teachings of Jesus are clearly to believe the truth to which Jesus testified.

- To believe "in a person" (God, Jesus, the Son) warrants some elaboration. Generally speaking, to *believe in* a person is to believe their representation of themselves. In this sense, to believe "in Jesus," would be to believe Jesus' claim that he had been sent by God, had come into this world to testify to the truth, and had done so. At a deeper level, to believe "in Jesus" is to believe while *abiding in* Jesus, while participating in his being.

- To believe "in the Son" (as distinct from Jesus) is to believe in Jesus' teaching concerning the Son of Man.

- To believe "in God" is to believe in the truth which is God. It is also to believe while abiding in God, while participating in God's being.

- To believe "in the light," is to believe that the "life" (eternal life) brought into being through the Word/truth has served and will serve as a light to others, enlightening them and enabling them to become children of light.

The Content of Belief

In earlier chapters we established the truth about God (in Chapters 2-4) and about ourselves (Chapters 5-7). But we have just begun to address the truth about what we are meant to be doing (Chapters 8-10), and will not address the truth about salvation until Chapter 11. Consequently, it is too early to specify what must be believed at this time. Nevertheless, it might be helpful to briefly review what we have established thus far.

The truth about God

There *is* an intention, a purpose behind existence. The purpose behind existence is to bring love into existence, to infuse this otherwise merely material world with love. God works through people in this world to bring about this purpose. He reveals the truth about existence directly to individuals and sends them to testify to others. God tells those whom he sends what they are to say and what they are to do. God draws people to the truth, and participates in their recognition and appropriation of the truth.

Alternatively, we could say that the truth (or the Word) reveals itself to people in this world, and sends them to testify to the truth to others. People (some people) are drawn to the truth, they recognize it when they hear it. These people adopt it as the truth about their own lives and go on to testify to others. Or, this time avoiding causal language, we could say that the truth occurs to people (some people), they adopt it as their own, testify to the truth to others, and bring their lives into accord with the truth. We are not able to account for these events, but behind them we see the work of a benevolent and transcendent influence.

The truth about ourselves

We are the intended recipients of eternal life, a transcendent state of being in relation to God. We have eternal life inasmuch as we believe, *and* bring our lives into accord with, the truth. We come to have eternal life (if it happens) in the "here and now," that is, during our otherwise ordinary lives in this world. To have eternal life is to abide in God and he in us, to be one with God, to be sanctified (made holy) by the truth and participate in the divinity of God. Although our material self will die, our transcendent self will live on eternally in God. We are invited and enabled by the truth to have eternal life in order that we might serve as agents of God (of the truth) in realizing the purpose behind existence: the bringing of love into being.

Anticipating the time when we will have established the complete truth, we might ask ourselves how will we know if the truth to which Jesus testified (as it is represented in the Gospel of John, or other documents) is true?

How Can We Know the Truth?

Nothing in and of this world, no combination of observable facts and logical analysis, can establish that there is such a thing as the truth behind existence, let alone what that truth is. Nevertheless, Jesus as he is represented in the Gospel, assures his listeners that they will be able to know the truth (*Then Jesus said to the Jews who had believed in him, "If you continue in my word, you are truly my disciples; and you will know the truth, and the truth will make you free."* 8:31-32). But how is it possible for us to know the truth?

Epistemology is a branch of philosophy that deals with the nature, methods, and limits of human knowledge. And so, in principle we could address the question of how we are able to know the truth by applying epistemological principles and methods to the task. Fortunately this won't be necessary because the Gospel of John contains its own epistemology, its own representation of how we are able to know the truth. Consequently, I propose that we look at what the Gospel reveals about the reliability of the several bases for belief that are represented in the Gospel.

Before proceeding, however, I should acknowledge that in the last few paragraphs I made a switch from *believing* the truth to *knowing* the truth. Is this legitimate? And what is the relationship between knowing and believing? Epistemologically speaking, to "know" something is to believe something that is true.[48] The truth behind existence is true by definition (if it exists), and so, to believe the truth is to know the truth, and *vice versa*. So, for the present application, the switch from believing to knowing is legitimate.

The Gospel of John contains evidence regarding its author's (and Jesus', as he is represented in the Gospel) understanding of the reliability of four candidate bases for belief:

- Signs: Miracles or other unusual events that could be seen as establishing Jesus' authority for testifying to the truth, and/or the truth of his testimony,

- Scripture: Passages from scripture that could be seen as establishing Jesus' authority for testifying, and/or establishing the truth of his testimony,

- Human testimony: The testimony of people that could be seen as establishing Jesus' authority for testifying, and/or the truth of his testimony, and

- Divine testimony: Communication of the truth directly from God to oneself.

---

[48] Some would reasonably add, "while having reasonable justification for believing," so as to disqualify uninformed opinions, guesses, and Pascalian wagers.

What does the text of the Gospel tell us about the
reliability of each of these bases for belief?

Signs

Signs - miraculous or otherwise impressive events that
could be understood to establish Jesus' authority and/or
the truth of his testimony - are featured in many of the
most memorable stories in the Gospel of John. These
stories include: the turning of water into wine at the
wedding in Cana (2:1-11), the healing of the son of a
royal official (4:46-54), the feeding of the five-thousand
with only five loaves and two fish (6:1-15), the restoration
of sight to a man who had been born blind (9:1-12), the
raising of Lazarus (11:1-44), and the appearances of the
resurrected Jesus to his remaining eleven male disciples
(20:19-29).

Within most of these stories, signs are said to lead to
belief on the part of the witnesses:

Jesus did this [the changing of water into wine],
*the first of his signs, in Cana of Galilee, and
revealed his glory; and his disciples believed in
him.* (2:11),

*When he was in Jerusalem during the Passover
festival, many believed in his name because they
saw the signs he was doing.* (2:23),

The father realized that this [the hour when his
son recovered] *was the hour when Jesus said to*

him, "Your son will live." So he himself believed, along with his whole household. (4:53),

When the people saw the sign that he had done [the feeding of the five-thousand], *they began to say, "This is indeed the prophet who is to come into the world."* (6:14),

"Never since the world began has it been heard that anyone opened the eyes of a person born blind. If this man [Jesus] *were not from God, he could do nothing."* (9:32-33),

Many of the Jews therefore, who had come with Mary and had seen what Jesus did [the raising of Lazarus], *believed in him.* (11:45), and

Thomas ["Doubting Thomas]" upon seeing the resurrected Jesus *answered him, "My Lord and my God!"* (20:28).

Nevertheless, within these stories we sometimes find evidence that Jesus did not believe that people's belief was genuine. Oddly enough, the first indication that signs might not provide a reliable basis for belief appears just after we have been told that *"many believed in his name because they saw the signs he was doing"* (2:23). In the very next verse the author tell us, <u>*But Jesus on his part would not entrust himself to them,*</u> *because he knew all people and needed no one to testify about anyone* ...(2:24). Similarly, after the feeding of the five thousand, the author tells us, *When the people saw the sign that he had done, they began to say, "This is indeed the prophet who is to come into the world."* (6:14). But then the author adds, *When Jesus realized that they were about to come and take him by force and make him king, he withdrew again to the mountain by himself.* (6:15). Here, the people who had seen the sign, and who had proclaimed him prophet, did not really understand Jesus, or what his life was about. And so Jesus chose to distance himself from them.

Are the responses of the participants in the Passover festival in Jerusalem and of the participants in the feeding of the five-thousand atypical? Not at all. Signs are frequently portrayed in John's Gospel as ineffective at bringing about either true understanding or belief. Early in the Gospel, at the beginning of Jesus' conversation with Nicodemus, Nicodemus says, *"Rabbi, we know that you are a teacher who has come from God; for no one can do the signs that you do apart from the presence of God."* (3:2). Jesus responds by telling Nicodemus that no one can see the kingdom of God without having been born from above, and that the workings of the spirit in this world are unpredictable. Nicodemus then asks, *"How can these things be?"* and Jesus answers, *"Are you a teacher of Israel, and yet you do not understand these things?"* (3:10). In spite of having witnessed, or having heard about and accepted as true, the signs that Jesus had done, Nicodemus was not familiar with the truth to which Jesus was testifying.

Not even seeing the raising of a man from the dead is sufficient to produce belief in Jesus (in the truth to which Jesus testified). Just after Lazarus has been raised from the dead the author tells us, *Many of the Jews therefore, who had come with Mary and had seen what Jesus did, believed in him.* (11:45). Others reported Jesus to the authorities: *But some of them went to the Pharisees and told them what he had done."* (11:46). And in the Gospel's account of Jesus' final public discourse, Jesus asks God to glorify his (God's) name, and a voice comes from heaven saying, *I have glorified it, and I will glorify it again."* (12:28). How does the audience react? The author tells us: *The crowd standing there heard it and said it was thunder. Others said, "An angel has spoken to him.* (12:29). Where some hear angels, others hear only noise.

More alarming evidence regarding the efficacy of signs (or lack thereof) can be found immediately after Jesus' last public discourse (12:20-36). The author notes that although Jesus had performed many signs in their presence, the people to whom he was speaking still did not believe:

> <u>*Although he had performed so many signs in their presence, they did not believe in him*</u>. *This was to fulfill the word spoken by the prophet Isaiah: "Lord, who has believed our message, and to whom has the arm of the Lord been revealed?"* (12:37-38).

The author goes on to claim that those who did not believe could not believe because, as Isaiah had written, *"He* [God] *has blinded their eyes and hardened their heart, so that they might not look with their eyes, and understand with their heart and turn and I would heal them."* (12:39-40). But some, even among the authorities, did believe Jesus but were afraid to admit it:

> *Nevertheless many, even among the authorities, believed him. But because of the Pharisees they did not confess it, for fear that they would be put out of the synagogue, for they loved human glory more than the glory that comes from God.* (12:42-43).

Jesus' attitude toward signs is revealed in several passages in the Gospel. On several occasions, he downplays signs as a basis for belief. After the episode of the feeding of the five-thousand and after Jesus has walked across the sea of Galilee, Jesus explains to a crowd that has been following him that it his words, *not* signs, to which they are (and undoubtedly should be) drawn: *Jesus answered them, "Very truly, I tell you, you are looking for me, not because you saw signs, but because you ate your fill of the loaves* [the truth, the word of God]. *"* (6:26) Still later in the Gospel the resurrected Jesus rebukes Thomas, the disciple who refused to believe without first seeing and touching Jesus' wounds, saying, *"Have you believed because you have seen me? Blessed are those who have not seen and yet have come to believe."* (20:29) Here the author - and Jesus, as he is represented in the Gospel - are telling us that signs are not necessary to belief and, moreover, to believe without having seen a sign is to be blessed.

A more fundamental question than what to make of signs is, are the signs in the Gospel of John signs at all? Often - perhaps always - stories that on the surface appear to represent signs are actually metaphorical representations of Jesus' testifying to the truth and/or the response of his audience to the truth. Thus, the story of the feeding of the five-thousand in Chapter 6 of the Gospel is a metaphorical representation of Jesus testifying to a large crowd gathered upon a mountain. The nourishment provided to the crowd is spiritual nourishment - the loaves of "bread" representing the word of God.

Similarly, the story of Jesus changing water into wine at the wedding in Cana (Chapter 2) is a metaphorical representation of Jesus producing a new (and true) representation of the truth - the truth about God, about who we are, about what we are meant to be doing, and about salvation. Thus, after drinking the wine made from water, the steward calls the bridegroom and exclaims, *"Everyone serves the good wine first, and the inferior wine after the guests have become drunk. But you have kept the good wine until now"* (2:10). The "inferior wine" is the then prevailing representation of the truth; the "good wine" is Jesus' better representation of the truth. The story of the man born blind (Chapter 9) is actually a metaphorical representation of a man who had been born "in the dark" about the truth suddenly having his eyes opened by Jesus' testimony. And the story of the raising of Lazarus is a metaphorical representation of a man who was "dead," or who had died, to the truth being brought back to "life," to eternal life, through Jesus' testimony.

Material signs do not provide a reliable basis for belief. True miracles - people being drawn to the truth, listening, hearing, coming to believe, and choosing to adopt the truth as their own - are not material facts; they cannot be seen or touched.

Scripture

Might scripture provide a reliable basis for coming to believe the truth? In John's Gospel we find frequent references to scripture, most notably to "the law" and to writings of the prophets. Events in Jesus' life are sometimes said to represent the "fulfillment" of scripture, and passages from scripture are sometimes cited by Jesus in support of his testimony. In most of the passages that refer to scripture, the connection between the passage and people coming to believe is not explicit. Most often the connection is implicit: if a passage from scripture corresponds to an event in Jesus' life then, by implication, the passage can be seen to support Jesus' authority and the truth of his testimony.

Explicit connections between scripture and belief *do* appear, however, in three passages in the Gospel. These passages relate to: (1) the cleansing of the temple, (2) the washing of the disciples' feet," and (3) the disciple's discovery of the empty tomb.

In the cleansing of the temple incident (verses 2:13-22), Jesus comes to the temple in Jerusalem where he finds people selling animals and changing money - normal activity at the temple when people come from afar with different currencies and wish to buy animals to offer for sacrifice. Jesus "makes a whip of cords," drives the animals out of the temple, overturns the tables of the money changers, and tells the dove sellers, *"Take these things out of here! Stop making my Father's house a marketplace!"* (2:16). The author then tells us that Jesus' disciples remembered that it was written, *"Zeal for your house will consume me."* (verse 2:17, loosely based on Psalm 69:9)

How did the disciples and/or author understand this fragment of scripture as it applied to what Jesus was doing in the temple? Whose zeal is it in verse 2:17? Is it Jesus' zeal for God's house, which will consume his full attention? Is it the money changers' and animal sellers' zeal for the sacrificial system that will consume (destroy) Jesus and his message? And, is being consumed by zeal a good thing or a bad thing in this context?

In any case, Jesus' audience at the temple asks, *"What sign can you give for doing this* [the cleansing of the temple]*?,"* and Jesus answers *"Destroy this temple, and in three days I will raise it up."* (2:19). His audience then asks, *"This temple has been under construction for forty-*

six years, and you will raise it up in three days?" (2:20), but the author explains that Jesus *"was speaking of the temple of his body."* (2:21) At this point, the author tells us, <u>*After he was raised from the dead, his disciples remembered that he had said this; and they believed the scripture and the word that Jesus had spoken.*</u> (2:22).

In the cleansing of the temple passage (2:13-22), Jesus' disciples do *not* come to believe the word that Jesus had spoken (the truth) on the basis of scripture. Rather, they come to believe the scripture and the word the Jesus had spoken much later, on the basis of their recognition that Jesus had been raised from the dead.

In the second passage connecting scripture to belief (13:1-20), Jesus hints that one of the disciples will betray him. In this passage, after Jesus has washed the disciples feet, Simon Peter asks Jesus to wash his hands and head too. Jesus replies, *"One who has bathed does not need to wash, except for the feet, but is entirely clean. And you are clean, though not all of you."* (13:10). The author then adds, *For he knew who was to betray him; for this reason he said, "Not all of you are clean."* (13:11). After explaining to the disciples that, in washing their feet, he was setting an example, he tells them.

> *"If you know these things, you are blessed if you do them. I am not speaking of all of you; I know whom I have chosen.* <u>*But it is to fulfill the scripture, 'The one who ate my bread has lifted his heel against me. I tell you this now before it*</u>

> *occurs, so that when it does occur, you may*
> *believe that I am he."* (13:17-19).

Here, Jesus links fulfillment of scripture to belief about Jesus, about who he is ("I am he" - the one who is to come into the world to testify to the truth.) In this passage, belief in Jesus comes about not on the basis of scripture but rather on the basis of Jesus having successfully predicted the betrayal before it happened. The successful prediction serves as a sign, a sign that Jesus is who is says he is.

The third explicit link between belief and scripture can be found late in the Gospel, when Peter and the Beloved Disciple ("the one whom Jesus loved") arrive at Jesus' empty tomb. Mary has already seen the stone removed from in front of the tomb and has run to tell Peter and the Beloved Disciple, *"They have taken the Lord out of the tomb, and we do not know where they have laid him."* (20:2). Peter and the Beloved Disciple then run to the tomb to see for themselves. The Beloved Disciple arrives first and notices the linen wrappings from Jesus' body lying inside. Peter enters the tomb and finds the cloth that had been on Jesus' head rolled up in a place by itself. The author then tells us,

> *Then the other disciple, who reached the tomb*
> *first, also went in and saw and believed; for as yet*
> *they did not understand the scripture, that he must*
> *rise from the dead.* (20:8-9).

This passage is somewhat puzzling in that it isn't clear
what the Beloved Disciple came to believe. Perhaps it
was that Jesus had risen from the dead. In any case, the
Beloved Disciple came to believe *not* on the basis of
scripture because "as yet they did not understand the
scripture. Rather, they came to believe on the basis of the
tomb being empty. The empty tomb led him to believe
that Jesus must rise from the dead, and this belief led him
to an understanding of scripture.[49] Thus, in none of the
passages that explicitly address both scripture and belief
does belief come about on the basis of scripture.

Scripture is, however, often cited in the Gospel to
establish Jesus' authority for testifying to the truth. In
response to a charge, by the Pharisees, that he has been
testifying on his own behalf, and thus his testimony is not
valid, Jesus wraps up his response by appealing to
scripture: *"In your law it is written that the testimony of
two witnesses is valid. I testify on my own behalf, and the
Father who sent me testifies on my behalf."* (8:17-18).
The clincher in this argument is not scripture, but the
testimony provided by God - testimony from outside
scripture, and which can only be heard by those who

[49] The scripture behind verse 20:9 is not quoted, paraphrased, or
identified in the NRSV translation itself, but a footnote *The New
Oxford Annotated Bible*, Oxford University Press, New York, 1991,
reads, "The O.T. [Old Testament] spoke of the resurrection of the
Messiah (Ps. 16:10)." However, nowhere in Ps. 16:10 do we find the
words Messiah *or* resurrection. The verse reads, "Therefore my
heart is glad, and my soul rejoices; my body also rests secure. For
you do not give me up to Sheol [a reference to death, or a place of
punishment for the wicked], or let your faithful one see the pit."
(Material in square brackets added for clarity.)

201

recognize the truth, and thus need no scripture to convince them.

Another passage that cites scripture in support of Jesus' authority comes just after his claim that, *"The Father and I are one"* (10:30). The Jews[50] then take up stones in order to stone him. Seeing this, Jesus tells them that he has done many good works from the Father, and asks for which of these are they going to stone him. The Jews answer, *"It is not for a good work that we are going to stone you, but for blasphemy, because you, though only a human being are making yourself God"* (8:33). Scripture comes into play when Jesus answers back:

> *"Is it not written in your law, 'I said, you are gods'? If those to whom the word of God came were called 'gods' - and the scripture cannot be annulled - can you say that one whom the Father has sanctified and sent into this world is blaspheming because I said, 'I am God's son'?"* (10:34-36).

---

[50] Here and elsewhere in the Gospel, and in this work, the term "the Jews": should be understood to refer to *some* of the Jews, or more particularly, to certain Jewish authorities. In fact, almost everyone in almost every story in the Gospel is a Jew, including Jesus, John the Baptist, Jesus' family (mother and brothers), Jesus' disciples, and Jesus' opponents. It may be interesting to note that the term "the Jews" appears 62 times in the Gospel. In all but two of these appearances, the term is used by the author of the Gospel. Jesus uses the term only twice, once in a positive way (verse 4:21) and one in a neutral (verse 3:33).

Scripture does play a role in Jesus' argument here, but the answer to Jesus' last question depends on whether you see Jesus as "one whom the Father has sanctified and sent into this world." And, of course, this is not determined from scripture. It depends on the Father testifying within oneself on Jesus' behalf, and on our recognizing his testimony.

Scripture is also cited, especially in the latter half of the Gospel, to account for the rejection of Jesus and his message by his own people (*He was in the world ... yet the world did not know him. He came to what was his own, and his own people did not accept him.* 1:10-11). When a crowd begins to complain about his having claimed to be "the bread of life," Jesus draws on scripture to explain their failure to believe:

> *Jesus answered them, "Do not complain among yourselves. No one can come to me unless drawn by the Father who sent me; and I will raise that person up on the last day. <u>It is written in the prophets, 'And they shall all be taught by God,' Everyone who has heard and learned from the Father comes to me.</u>"* (6:43-45).

In this passage Jesus is suggesting that people in the crowd can't come to him for the truth because they have not heard and learned from the Father.[51]

---

[51] The passage seems to contradict itself in the sense that if *all* are taught by God then they all would have heard and learned from the Father, and would be drawn by the Father and come to Jesus. But

For Jesus, the failure to believe is the people's failure to hear and understand. But, for the author of the Gospel, the people's failure to believe was an intentional act of God:

> *Although he* [Jesus] *had performed so many signs in their presence, they did not believe in him. This was to fulfill the word spoken by the prophet Isaiah: "Lord, who has believed our message, and to whom has the arm of the Lord been revealed?"* (12:37-38; based on Isaiah 53:1)

> *And so they could not believe, because Isaiah also said, "He has blinded their eyes, and hardened their heart, so that they might not look with their eyes and understand with their heart and turn - and I would heal them."* (12:39-40; loosely based on Isaiah 6:9-10)

However, in light of God's purpose, which is to bring love into being by revealing the truth and sending people to testify, it is unlikely that God would blind people and harden their hearts. Isaiah's and the author of the Gospel's view here, is based on the assumption that everything that happens represents God's will. Not everything that happens is God's will, but God (the truth)

---

apparently *some* haven't, and they are doing the complaining. Apparently the "all" means all those who are drawn to Jesus by the Father. The contradictions are dissolved if we read the passage tautologically, that is, if we understand that to come to Jesus *is* to be drawn by the Father, *is* to be taught by God, and *is* to hear and learn from the Father.

does have a way of bending everything that happens toward its will.

The notion that scripture might be a reliable basis for believing is somewhat undercut by the fact that scripture can be, and is, referenced to support the points of view of both Jesus *and* of his opponents. In the Gospel of John, Jesus' opponents cite scripture to make the case that (a) the woman caught in adultery should be stoned (8:3-5), (b) that Jesus couldn't be the Messiah and yet be "lifted up" (crucified) because, in the law, the Messiah lasts forever (12:34-35), and (c) that Jesus should be killed by the Romans because he had claimed to be the Son of God (*The Jews answered him* [Pilate], *"We have a law, and according to that law he ought to die because he has claimed to be the Son of God."*(19:7).

Scripture as a basis for belief is further undercut by the fact that, in the Gospel, Jesus does not feel bound by scripture. This can be seen in the story of the woman caught in adultery. It can also be seen in the story of the man born blind, in which Jesus performs a healing on the Sabbath (*Now it was the sabbath day when Jesus made the mud and opened his eyes.* 9:14). Some of the Pharisees object, saying, *"This man is not from God, for he does not observe the sabbath."* (9:16).

Jesus' attitude toward scripture is most clearly revealed in his comment to those who reject his testimony, *"You search the scriptures because you think*

205

that in them you have eternal life; and it is they that testify *on my behalf. Yet you refuse to come to me to have life."* (5:39). It is not scripture but rather the word of God, the truth to which Jesus testified, that can bring us to eternal life.

Human testimony

That human testimony *can* lead to belief is a basic premise of the Gospel of John. In the Gospel of John Jesus is represented as having come into this world for the purpose of testifying to the truth (18:37). And throughout the Gospel we read of others who testify so that we might believe:

- John the Baptist (... *He came as a witness to* *testify to the light, so that all might believe* *through him.* 1:7),

- Jesus and his colleagues (*"Very truly, I tell you,* *we speak of what we know and testify to what we* *have seen; yet you do not receive our testimony. If* *I have told you about earthly things and you do* *not believe, how can you believe when I tell you* *about heavenly things?"* 3:11),

- The one (anyone) who comes from heaven (*The* *one who comes from heaven is above all. ... He* *testifies to what he has seen and heard ...* 3:31), and

- A crowd (*So the crowd that had been with him when he called Lazarus out of the tomb ... continued to testify.* 12:17).

The author (or a final editor) of the Gospel attached considerable weight to the testimony of one person in particular, a person said to have been an eyewitness to Jesus' life and death. Immediately after describing a scene at the crucifixion (*... one of the soldiers pierced Jesus' side with a spear, and at once blood and water came out.* 19:34) the author then tells us in an aside, *He who saw this has testified so that you might believe. His testimony is true, and he* [or, a footnote in the NRSV translation tells us, *there is one who*] *knows that he tells the truth.* (19:35). The person "who saw this" in verse 19:35 is later identified as "the disciple whom Jesus loved." And in the final chapter of the Gospel, the author tells us, *This is the disciple who is testifying to these things and has written them, and we know that his testimony is true.* (21:24). Note that, in this verse the author adds his own and his colleague's testimony on top of that of "the Beloved Disciple."

The Gospel also speaks of people coming to believe through human testimony. In his final, intercessory prayer on behalf of his disciples, Jesus speaks of *"those who will believe in me through their* [the disciples']*word"* (17:20). And the author (or perhaps John the Baptist) speaks of those who accept the testimony of "the one who comes from above" (*Whoever has accepted his testimony has certified this, that God is true.* 3:33). More specifically, the men of Samaria accept the testimony of a Samaritan woman who had conversed with Jesus at Jacob's well (*Many Samaritans from the city believed in him because of the woman's testimony, "He told me everything that I have ever done."* (4:39). The Samaritan woman's belief at this point appears to have been based on the fact that Jesus knew everything that she had ever done, and the Samaritans (presumably men) seem to have come to believe on the basis of her testimony. But, after spending some time with Jesus themselves, the Samaritans came to believe on the basis of Jesus' own words (*They said to the woman, "It is no longer because of what you said that we believe, for we have heard for ourselves, and we know that this is truly the Savior of the world."* (4:42).

While human testimony is sometimes represented as effective at bringing about belief, at other times it is represented as ineffective. When Jesus attempts to tell Nicodemus about how it is that one can see the kingdom of God, Nicodemus asks, *"How can these things be?"* (3:9), Jesus answers,

> *"Are you a teacher of Israel, and yet do not understand these things? Very truly, I tell you,* <u>we</u> [Jesus and his colleagues] *speak of what we know and testify to what we have seen; yet you do not receive our testimony."* (3:10-11).

Believing

And later in the same chapter, the author (or perhaps John the Baptist[52]) laments, *The one who is from heaven is above all.* ... *He testifies to what he has seen and heard, yet no one accepts his testimony.* (3:31-32). The blanket statement here is hyperbolic. In the very next verse we are told that some do accept his testimony (*Whoever has accepted his testimony has certified this, that God is true."* (3:33).

Jesus, as he is represented in the Gospel, distrusted human testimony, even his own. As he put it,

> *"If I testify about myself, my testimony is not true. There is another who testifies on my behalf, and I know that his testimony to me is true. You sent messengers to John, and he testified to the truth. Not that I accept such human testimony, but I say these things so that you may be saved."* (5:31-34).

This passage has it both ways. Jesus disavows his own testimony, while testifying. And Jesus cites the Baptist's testimony, while saying that he does not accept such testimony.

Divine Testimony

Human testimony is not sufficient by itself to lead a person to belief in the truth. Even the testimony of one

---

[52] Verses 3:31-36 are attributed to the author of the Gospel in the NRSV and the NAB versions of the Gospel. They are attributed to the Baptist in the NIV and NAS.

who comes from above is not enough. Something else is needed. And what that something is is suggested in Jesus' argument with the Pharisees: *"In your law it is written that the testimony of two witnesses is valid. I testify on my own behalf, and the Father who sent me testifies on my behalf."* (8:17-18). The clincher in this argument is not a sign, not scripture, not human testimony, but rather the testimony provided by God, divine testimony.

The earliest indication in the Gospel that something beyond human testimony might be involved in a person's coming to know the truth appears in the prologue to the Gospel, wherein we find, *But to all who received him, who believed in his name, he gave power to become children of God, who were born, not of blood or of the will of the flesh or of the will of man, but of God.* (1:12-13). Those who received Jesus (in particular, the truth that he represented) and believed in his name were those who were born of God.

Essentially the same point is made early in the main narrative, when Jesus tells Nicodemus, *"... no one can see the kingdom of God without being born from above."* (3:3). The Greek word translated here as "kingdom" could also be translated as "reign." In any case, the kingdom/reign of God is that part or aspect of this world that has come under the influence of God (of the truth which *is* God). To "see the kingdom of God," is to recognize the manifestation of the transcendent (of God, truth, Spirit, ...) behind otherwise ordinary circumstances or events in this world. In verse 3:3 Jesus is telling Nicodemus - and the author is telling us - that to be able to recognize the kingdom of God in this world one must be born from above.

A person's origin in the transcendent explains the person's ability to recognize the truth. Those who have been born of God - or, equivalently, have come from above - have seen and heard the truth directly from God. As the author (or John the Baptist) put it, *The one who comes from above is above all ... The one who comes from heaven is above all. He testifies to what he has seen and heard ...* (3:31-32). Lest we think of "the one who comes from heaven" as being one particular person, Jesus includes his colleagues among those who have "seen" the truth in God's presence (*"Very truly, I tell you, we speak of what we know and testify to what we have seen ..."* (3:11). The truth is that *all* who are from God hear the words of God (*"... If I tell the truth, why do you not believe me? <u>Whoever is from God hears the words of God</u>. The reason you do not hear them is that you are not from God."* (8:46-47). They have all been taught by God, even before coming to Jesus for the truth (*It is written in the prophets, '<u>And they shall all be taught by God</u>.' Everyone who has heard and learned from the Father comes to me."* (6:45).

Having heard the truth directly from God, a person is able to recognize (re-know) the truth when they hear (or read) it from other sources. The testimony of others can remind people of that which they may have forgotten, or that about which they have become confused. That is how we might explain it from a causal perspective. From a tautological perspective, to be born of God *is* to receive the truth from God; to receive the truth directly from God *is* to be born of God. And to receive the truth from God and be born of God can happen simultaneously with our recognizing the truth in the testimony of another. To put it more simply, the truth can dawn on us, and we can be born of God, while listening to the testimony of others.

God does not just reveal the truth to people and thereafter abandon them to fend for themselves. God continues to reveal the truth to them. In defending his healing of a sick man on the sabbath, Jesus defended his actions by explaining, *"My Father is still working, and I also am working."* (5:17). God continued to work within Jesus (*"Do you not believe that I am in the Father and the Father is in me? The words that I say to you I do not speak on my own; but the Father who dwells in me does his works."* (14:10). And Jesus expected that God - in the guise of the Advocate (aka the Holy Spirit, the Spirit of truth) - would continue to testify to the truth:

> *"If you love me, you will keep my commandments.*
> *And I will ask the Father, and he will give you*
> *another Advocate, to be with you forever. This is*
> *the Spirit of truth, whom the world cannot receive,*
> *because it neither sees him nor knows him. You*
> *know him, because he abides with you, and he will*
> *be in you."* (14:15-17) and

"...the Advocate, the Holy Spirit, whom the Father will send in my name, will teach you everything, and remind you of all that I have said to you." (14:26).

Conclusion

As it is represented in the Gospel of John, the only reliable basis for true belief - for coming to know the truth to which Jesus testified - is divine testimony: direct communication of the truth from God, from the transcendent to the believer. Human testimony can remind a person of the truth which he or she had already received from God - but, even in this case, direct divine testimony to the validity (truthfulness) of the human testimony is necessary.

Is Believing Voluntary?

After Jesus tells the crowd that has followed him across the Sea of Galilee that they have followed him not because they saw signs, but because they had eaten their fill of the loaves (i.e., had heard the truth from him), he goes on to tell them: *"Do not work for the food that perishes, but for the food that endures for eternal life, which the Son of Man will give you. For it is on him that God the Father has set his seal."* (6:27). The crowd then asks, *"What must we do to perform the works of God?"* (6:28), and Jesus replies, *"This is the work of God, that you believe in him whom he has sent."* (6:29). Jesus' reply might seem a little off. The crowd had asked what *they* (the members of the crowd) must do to have eternal life, but Jesus seems to be speaking of something that *God* does. Is our coming to believe a work of God or of man? Perhaps of both. A person's coming to believe is the work of God (of the truth) within the person; at the same time, recognition and appropriation of the truth is the work of man.

There is no way to account for a person coming to believe and to act on the truth. As Jesus put it, *"... 'You must be born from above.' The wind blows where it chooses and you hear the sound of it, but you do not know where it comes from or where it goes. So it is with everyone who is born of the spirit."* (3:7b-8). Sometimes people recognize the truth when they hear it from others. Sometimes people recognize the truth when they witness evil or indifference in this world, and realize that it is very wrong. Jesus anticipated that this would be the case when he was "lifted up" on the cross:

> *So Jesus said, "When you have lifted up the Son of Man, then you will realize that I am he, and that I do nothing on my own, but I speak these things as the Father instructed me. And the one who sent me is with me; he has not left me alone, for I always do what is pleasing to him."* (8:28-29), and

Believing

*"And I, when I am lifted up from the earth, will
draw all people to myself."* (12:32).

Coming to believe happens to, or perhaps better,
within a person. And it often comes as a surprise to the
person. People come to recognize the truth suddenly and
inexplicably throughout the Gospel of John. John the
Baptist sees Jesus coming toward him and abruptly
declares, *"Here is the Lamb of God who takes away the
sin of the world!"* (1:29). He then explains, *"I saw the
Spirit descending from heaven like a dove, and it
remained on him. I myself didn't know him. ..."* (1:32-
33). When Jesus says of Nathanael, whom he is meeting
for the first time, *"Here is truly an Israelite in whom
there is no deceit"* (1:47b), Nathanael suddenly blurts out,
*"Rabbi, you are the Son of God! You are the King of
Israel!"* (1:49). The man blind from birth suddenly
recovers his sight (*"The man called Jesus made mud,
spread it on my eyes, and said to me, 'Go to Siloam and
wash.' Then I went and washed and received my sight."*
(9:11). Martha (sister of Lazarus) - having been asked by
Jesus whether she believes what he has been saying about
dying but never dying - instantly recognizes Jesus' words
as the truth, and blurts out, *"Yes, Lord, I believe that you
are the Messiah, the Son of God, the one coming into the
world."* (11:27). And the Beloved Disciple, upon seeing
the empty tomb suddenly understands the scripture that
Jesus must rise from the dead: *"Then the other disciple,
who reached the tomb first, also went in, and he saw and
believed ..."* (20:8).

We can't *decide* to believe the truth behind existence - we either believe or we don't. Of course we can choose to speak and act *as if* we believed, but our hearts and our minds won't really be in it until the truth dawns on us. However, for the truth to dawn on us is to do so by the grace of God, the grace mentioned in the prologue to the Gospel, *From his fullness we have all received, grace upon grace. The law indeed was given through Moses; grace and truth came through Jesus Christ.* (1:16-17).

Believing is not voluntary; the truth either occurs to us or it doesn't. Nevertheless there are things we can do to facilitate (cooperate with) our coming to know the truth. This may be why Jesus urged his listeners to work for the food that endures for eternal life. What we *can* do is:

- Take seriously our sense (if we have it) that existence is, or might be, about something, rather than nothing (or, equivalently that there is a purpose behind existence, or that what we do really does matter).

- Search for the truth about existence where we have a hunch it might best be found.

- Study promising sources of the truth, and work to establish what they are saying and what they mean.

- Adjust, as necessary, what we find in the sources so as to come up with an understanding of the truth that makes sense and strikes us as true.

- Work out the implications of our understanding of the truth for our own life.

- Put our understanding of the truth into practice.

In the process, the truth might just dawn on us.

Is Believing Enough?

Believing the truth is necessary for eternal life, and for becoming children of God. But is believing, by itself, enough? In view of the many verses in the Gospel that link belief with eternal life, one might conclude that it is. But the truth is that believing, by itself, is *not* enough. In fact, there is no such thing as believing "by itself." This is because to believe the truth is to believe that one must do two things: love others and testify to the truth. By loving others (all others) and testifying to the truth, we participate in the kingdom of God and in realizing the purpose behind existence.

We will examine the need to love, as it is represented in the Gospel of John, in the next chapter (Chapter 9 Loving), and the need to testify in Chapter 10 (Testifying).

Points to Keep in Mind

- **In order to have eternal life and participate effectively in realizing the purpose behind** existence (the bringing of love into being), a person must believe (understand and recognize as true) the truth.

- A reliable basis for believing the truth behind existence cannot be found in signs, or scripture, or human testimony by itself. The only reliable basis for believing is divine testimony: communication of or confirmation of the truth by God.

- Believing is not voluntary. We cannot not decide to believe; we either do or we don't. However, if we are drawn to the truth we can pursue, and form our own understanding of, the truth.

- Believing by itself is not enough to secure eternal life and, more importantly, contribute to realizing the purpose behind existence.

Chapter 9

LOVING

"I give you a new commandment, that you love one another. Just as I have loved you, you also should love one another. By this everyone will know that you are my disciples, if you have love for one another." (13:34-35)

In the Gospel of John Jesus repeatedly calls on his disciples (followers) to love one another. Having pronounced his "new commandment" to love in verses 13:34-35, Jesus repeats it in verses 15:12 (*"This is my commandment, that you love one another as I have loved you."*) and 15:17 (*"I am giving you these commands so that you may love one another."*). Jesus' "new" commandment is not particularly new[53]; what is new is that Jesus gives his disciples no other commandment.

The particular wording of Jesus' commandment to his disciples, however, raises an important question. In each instance Jesus tells his disciples to love "one another." He doesn't say, love everyone. Did he mean that his disciples are to love *only* other disciples?

---

[53] In the Old Testament (Leviticus 19:18), the Lord (God) tells Moses, *You shall not take vengeance or bear a grudge against any of your people, but you shall love your neighbor as yourself; I am the Lord."*

In this chapter I will first present the case for that disciples of Jesus are meant to love all others, and unconditionally. I will then identify passages in the Gospel that suggest otherwise (problem passages) and draw conclusions based on consistency with the Gospel as a whole. Finally, I will identify specific values and acts that are represented in the Gospel as being consistent with divine love - the love that has its origin in God.

The Case for Universal and Unconditional Love

The topic of love is first mentioned in the Gospel of John when Jesus tells Nicodemus (or the author of the Gospel tells the reader), *"God so loved the world that he gave his only Son, so that everyone who believes in him may not perish but may have eternal life."* (3:16). This verse is immediately followed by an alternative way of making essentially the same point: *"Indeed, God did not send the Son into the world to condemn the world, but in order that the world might be saved through him."* (3:17). God's love for the world was expressed in his sending of Jesus to testify to the truth to everyone so that they *might* have eternal life and be saved. Whether any individual comes to have eternal life and be saved depends on his or her response to the truth. It is important to note that, in these verses, God loved the world (everyone), without regard to who would and who would not come to believe in the Son. In these verses, God's love can be seen as both universal and unconditional.

That God offers the possibility of eternal life to everyone is first expressed in the prologue to the Gospel. Having said that life had come into being through the Word, the author goes on to tell us that this life (eternal life) serves to enlighten all people (… *and the life was the light of all people* 1:4) and, referring to Jesus, *The true light, which enlightens everyone, was coming into the world."* (1:9).

Even the "dead" - those who are dead to the truth - can hear and recognize the truth and come to have eternal life. In the Gospel, Jesus tells his listeners, *"Very truly, I tell you, anyone who hears my word and believes him who sent me has eternal life, and does not come under judgment, but has passed from death to life."* (5:24) and *"Very truly, I tell you, the hour is coming, and is now here, when the dead will hear the voice of the Son of God, and those who hear will live."* (5:25). It has happened, and there is no reason to believe that it won't go on happening. God does not, and cannot, compel recognition of the truth, but he can and does offer the truth to all.

Jesus' love

God's love is the model for Jesus' love: *"As the Father has loved me, so I have loved you; abide in his love. If you keep my commandments, you will abide in my love, just as I have kept my Father's commandments and abide in his love."* (15:9-10). In this passage, Jesus instructs his followers to abide in God's love, and in his own. To abide in God's and Jesus' love is to be loved *by*

God and Jesus, and to love *as* they loved. To abide in this sense, the disciples of Jesus must love others universally and unconditionally.

Jesus' practice of testifying to everyone - not only his fellow Jews, but also Samaritans and Gentiles - and his willingness to die to bring the truth to everyone (*"And I, when I am lifted up from the earth, will draw all people to myself. ..."* 12:32), indicate that Jesus' love too was universal. That it was unconditional is suggested in his reluctance to judge others, even those who did not "keep his words": *"I do not judge anyone who hears my words and does not keep them, for I came not to judge the world, but to save the world."* (12:47). Jesus' intent was to save not only the already saved (his followers) but everyone.

God's purpose

Since God's ultimate purpose - the purpose behind existence - is to bring love into being in this otherwise merely material world (see Chapter 3), for disciples of Jesus to limit their love in any way would be inconsistent with God's purpose. To feel and act toward others with anything less than love would testify not to the truth, but rather to the values of this world.

Support from other Gospels

The evidence cited thus far supports the proposition that Jesus' disciples are meant to love *all* others - universally and unconditionally. But, for an explicit call for all-encompassing love on the part of the disciples, we would need to turn to other early Christian writings, such as the Gospels of Matthew, Mark, and Luke, and the Epistles (letters) of Paul.

- The NRSV translation, Matthew 5:43-45 reads, *"You have heard that it was said, 'You shall love your neighbor and hate your enemy.' But I say to you, <u>Love your enemies and pray for those who persecute you, so that you may be children of your Father in heaven</u>; for he makes his sun rise on the evil and the good, and sends rain on the righteous and unrighteous."*

- In the NRSV translation of Mark 12:29-31, Jesus gives his version of the greatest commandments: *Jesus answered, "The first is, 'Hear, O Israel: the Lord our God, the Lord is one; you shall love the Lord your God with all your heart, and with all your soul, and with all you mind, and with all your strength.' The second is this, "<u>You shall love your neighbor as yourself</u>.' There is no other commandment greater than these."* Here, Jesus recognizes two commandments together as the greatest.

- The NRSV translation, Luke 6:27-28 reads, *"But I say to you that listen, Love your enemies, do good to those who hate you, bless those who curse you, pray for those who abuse you."*

- In the NRSV translation of his Letter to the Galatians, Paul summarizes the entirety of Jewish law in a single commandment: *"For the whole law is summed up in a single commandment, "You shall love your neighbor as yourself."* (Galatians 5:14)

Why then "one another"?

If Jesus really meant that his followers should love everyone, universally and unconditionally, then why did he repeatedly say (or why does the author represent him as having said) that they should love "one another" instead of "everyone"? That he said "one another" suggests that there may have been discord among Jesus followers. Perhaps there were differences over who was the most important disciple, or who Jesus loved most, or the interpretation of Jesus' words.

Another New Testament document, The First Letter of John (generally referred to as 1 John), written years after Jesus' death, suggests that serious differences had developed among Jesus' followers. The second chapter of 1 John speaks of believers hating other believers, and having split with the community:

> *Whoever says, "I am in the light," while hating a brother or sister,[1] is still in the darkness. Whoever loves a brother or sister[1] lives in the light, and in such a person[2] there is no cause for stumbling. But whoever hates another believer[1] is in the darkness, walks in the darkness, and does not*

know the way to go, because the darkness has brought on blindness. (1 John 2:9-11).

And in that same chapter,

Children, it is the last hour! As you have heard that antichrist is coming, so now <u>many antichrists have come</u>. From this we know that it is the last hour. <u>They went out from us, but they did not belong to us; for if they had belonged to us, they would have remained with us.</u> But by going out they made it plain that none of them belongs to us. (1 John 2:18-19).

And later, in chapter 4,

<u>*Those who say, "I love God," and hate their brothers or sisters are liars; for those who do not love a brother or sister whom they have seen, cannot love God whom they have not seen.*</u> [21] *The commandment we have from him is this: those who love God must love their brothers and sister also.* (1 John 4:20-21).

If there had been discord among the disciples, Jesus would likely have wanted them to set a better example to outsiders. He would expect them to love *at least* each other.

Problem passages

Some passages in the Gospel of John seem to suggest that God's love depends on a person's behavior. In these

225

passages, reasons are given for God's love. For instance, *"For this reason <u>the Father loves me</u> [Jesus], <u>because I lay down my life in order to take it up again.</u>"* (10:17). Here it would appear that God's love for Jesus depended on Jesus' laying down of his life. Reasons are also given for God's love for Jesus' disciples:

> *"<u>They who have my commandments and keep them</u> are those who love me; and those who love me <u>will be loved by my Father</u>, and I will love them and reveal myself to them." Judas (not Iscariot) said to him, "Lord, how is it that you will reveal yourself to us, and not to the world?" Jesus answered him, "<u>Those who love me will keep my word, and my Father will love them</u>, and we will come to them and make our home with them."* (14:21-23).

Conditional love also appears to be at play when Jesus tells his disciples, *"... for <u>the Father himself loves you, because you have loved me and have believed that I came from God.</u>"* (16:27).

However, the notion that God's love for Jesus was conditional is directly contradicted in verse 17:24, where we find Jesus saying, *"Father, I desire that those also, whom you have given me, may be with me where I am, to see my glory, which you have given me because <u>you loved me before the foundation of the world.</u>"* As Jesus understood it, God loved him before the foundation of the world, before any conditions could have been met. And the notion that God's love for others was (and might still be) conditional is at odds with verse 3:16, wherein we find that God loved the world - including, presumably, the people in it - even before they could have known, believed, and loved Jesus.

Inasmuch as (a) the bringing of love into being in this world is God's ultimate purpose, (b) there are no passages in the Gospel of John that suggest that God does *not* love non-believers or those who fail to keep Jesus' word, (c) and the statements that suggest conditionality are contradicted within the text, the understanding that best fits the Gospel as a whole is that God's love was and is both universal and unconditional.

The Nature of Love

Just what would constitute loving others is not explicitly defined in the Gospel. We have the general instruction to the disciples to love *as* Jesus loved (verses 13:34 and 15:12), but in what way or ways *did* Jesus love? The answer to this question can best be determined by looking at what Jesus does.

Forgiveness

In the Gospel of John Jesus offers forgiveness to, and refuses to condemn, those who transgress the law (religious law). And he suggests that others do so as well. This point is made in the story of the woman caught in adultery (verses 8:2-11). In this story the scribes and Pharisees point out that Moses had commanded that such women be stoned, and they ask Jesus what he thinks should be done. Jesus answers, *"Let him among you who is without sin be the first to throw a stone at her."* (8:7). In effect he is saying, "do not stone her, because - let's face it - none of us is without sin." The scribes and Pharisees, recognizing the truth of Jesus' words, skulk away (*When they heard it, they went away, one by one, beginning with the elders ...* 8:9). Jesus then asks the woman, *"Has no one condemned you?"*, and when she answers, *"No one Sir"*, Jesus replies, *"Neither do I condemn you ...."* (8:10-11).

Non-violence

Jesus' response to the situation posed by the woman caught in adultery is in keeping with his recognition that violence has no place in his kingdom, the kingdom of God. After being asked by Pontius Pilate, *"Are you the King of the Jews?"*, Jesus declares, *"My kingdom is not from this world. If my kingdom were from this world, my followers would be fighting to keep me from being handed over to the Jews. But as it is, my kingdom is not from here."* (18:33-36). Earlier in the Gospel, Jesus had warned his followers about the violence to be done to them in God's name,

> *"They will put you out of the synagogues. Indeed, an hour is coming when those who kill you will think that by doing so they are offering worship to*

Loving

God. And they will do this because they have not
known the Father or me." (16:2-3)

Respect for others, whatever their social standing

Jesus extended respect to others without regard for
their social standing. He demonstrated his respect for his
disciples by washing their feet:

> *... during supper Jesus, knowing that the Father*
> *had given all things into his hands, and that he*
> *had come from God and was going to God, got up*
> *from the table, took off his outer robe, and tied a*
> *towel around himself. Then he poured water into*
> *a basin and began to wash the disciples feet and to*
> *wipe them with the towel that was tied around*
> *him.* (13:2-5).

But, in doing so, he ran into objections from Peter:

> *He came to Simon Peter, who said to him, "Lord*
> *are you going to wash my feet?" Jesus answered,*
> *"You do not know now what I am doing, but later*
> *you will understand." Peter said to him, "You*
> *will never wash my feet." Jesus answered,*
> *"Unless I wash you, you have no share with me."*
> (13:6-10).

Unless Peter allows Jesus to wash his feet - that is, unless
he recognizes that we are to have, and to demonstrate,

respect for others, we have no share with Jesus, no share in God, no share in the kingdom of God.

Not sure that his disciples have understood the significance of what he has just done, Jesus goes on to explain,

> *"Do you know what I have done to you? You call me Teacher and Lord - and you are right, for that is what I am. So if I, your Lord and Teacher, have washed you feet, you also ought to wash one another's feet. For I have set for you an example, that you also should do as I have done to you."*
> (13:12-15).

The point is that we are to care for each other, and no one is above washing another's feet.

Self-sacrifice

Jesus was also willing to die in order to bring the truth to those who would listen. In his "good shepherd discourse " (verses 10:1-18), Jesus likened himself to a good shepherd, a shepherd who is willing to lay down his life for his sheep:

> *"I am the good shepherd. The good shepherd lays down his life for his sheep. The hired hand, who is not the shepherd and does not own the sheep, sees the wolf coming and leaves the sheep and*

> *runs away ... The hired hand runs away because a*
> *hired hand does not care for the sheep. <u>I am the</u>*
> <u>*good shepherd. ... And I lay down my life for the*</u>
> <u>*sheep.*</u> *I have other sheep that do not belong to*
> *this fold. I must bring them also, and they will*
> *listen to my voice. ..."* (10:11-16).

Jesus did not run away when he saw the wolves coming.
In its immediate context, i.e., verses 10:11-16 the
emphasis is on Jesus' love for his "sheep," which is
evidenced by his willingness to lay down his life in order
to lead them to the truth. And, as Jesus' understood it, to
lay down of one's life for others is the greatest form of
love (*"No one has greater love than this, to lay down
one's life for one's friends."* 15:13).

The laying down one's life *can* "bear fruit" (in this
case, lead people to the truth):

> *"The hour has come for the Son of Man to be*
> *glorified. Very truly, I tell you, <u>unless a grain of</u>*
> <u>*wheat falls into the earth and dies, it remains just*</u>
> <u>*a single grain; but if it dies, it bears much fruit.*</u>
> *Those who love their life lose it, and those who*
> *hate their life in this world will keep it for eternal*
> *life. Whoever serves me must follow me, and*
> *where I am, there will my servant be also."*
> (12:23-26a).

But, do we *need to* die in order to bear fruit? Yes, but not
necessarily in the literal sense. More often, we will need

Loving

to die to (let go of our attachment to) the things and values of this world. As Jesus put it, "those who love their life will lose it, and those who hate their life in this world will keep it." Jesus' (or the author's or editor's) choice of the word "hate" here is hyperbolic. There is no room in the truth for hate. Rather than hating our lives in this world, we are called by the truth to choose between (a) living in accord with the values of this, the material world and (b) living in accord with the truth.

In general, to reject the values of this world in favor of the truth can be dangerous. Recognizing this, Jesus warns his disciples that they will be subject to the world's hatred:

> *"If you belonged to the world, the world would love you as its own. Because you do not belong to the world, but I have chosen you out of the world - therefore the world hates you."* (15:19).

It is not easy to make the right choice and stay with it. We are easily seduced by the values of this world because of the social reinforcement that it brings. We can easily find ourselves loving the wrong things.

Misplaced Love

In the Gospel, Jesus speaks of several forms of what I think of as misplaced love: love of those things of this world, things that can separate us from the truth, and thus from eternal life and salvation. Early in the Gospel of John, Jesus refers to people who "love darkness":

Loving

> *"And this is the judgment, that the light has come
> into the world, and <u>the people loved darkness
> rather than light</u> because their deeds were evil.
> For all who do evil hate the light and do not come
> to the light, so that their deeds may not be
> exposed."* (3:19-20).

Who are these people, the people who loved darkness?
Presumably they are the same people that are referred to a
few verses earlier, people who are "condemned already":
*"Indeed, God did not send the Son into the world to
condemn the world. ... Those who believe in him are not
condemned; but those who do not believe are condemned
already ..."* (3:17-18).

Another form of misplaced love is the love of human
glory, glorification by others. As Jesus put it, *"I do not
accept glory from human beings. ... <u>How can you believe
when you accept glory from one another</u> and do not seek
the glory that comes from the one alone who is God?*
(5:41-44). The love of human glory can be found even in
the heart of religious orthodoxy. The author of the
Gospel tells us that many believed in Jesus, but were
afraid to confess it for fear they would be put out of the
synagogue:

> *Nevertheless many, even of the authorities,
> believed in him. But because of the Pharisees they
> did not confess it, for fear that they would be put
> out of the synagogue; for <u>they loved human glory</u>*

more than the glory that comes from God. (12:42-
43).

Human glory is the recognition and acclaim given to us in
our various social contexts: business, politics, religion,
entertainment ... Human glory can blind us to the word,
to the truth. To accept human glory is to "belong to the
world" rather than to the truth.

True love

Jesus' behavior in the Gospel suggests that the love
called for by the truth encompasses:

- not condemning but forgiving others,

- refusing to participate in violence, particularly in
  the name of God,

- behaving respectfully to others without regard to
  their social standing, and

- sacrificing oneself - being willing to die - literally
  or to the things of this world - in order to bring the
  truth to others, and with the truth, the possibility
  of eternal life and salvation

Love as Testimony

When Jesus gave his disciples the commandment to
love one another he concluded by telling them, *"By this
everyone will know that you are my disciples, if you have*

Loving

love for one another." (13:35). Here the emphasis is on
everyone being able to recognize the disciples as true
disciples of Jesus. At the same time, verse 13:35 testifies
to the nature of the truth to which Jesus testified: love
trumps every other consideration.

Was the disciple's testimony necessary? Yes. And
our testimony is necessary too, as will be made clear in
the next chapter.

Points to Keep in Mind

- **Jesus introduced a "new" commandment: that
  we love one another. What is new in this
  commandment is that it is Jesus'** *only*
  commandment.

- **We are meant to love others as God and Jesus
  love(d): universally and unconditionally.**

- **Our love for others is to encompass forgiveness,
  non-violence, respect for others, and a
  willingness to die - literally or figuratively - if
  necessary in order to bring the truth to others.**

- **Love for others is the indicator of true
  discipleship. Love trumps everything.**

Chapter 10

TESTIFYING

The one who comes from above is above all; the one who is of the earth belongs to the earth and speaks of earthly things. The one who comes from heaven is above all. He testifies to what he has seen and heard, yet no one accepts his testimony. Whoever has accepted his testimony has certified this, that God is true. (3:31-33)

To know the truth is to recognize one's personal responsibility to testify to the truth. This element of the truth is introduced early in the prologue of the Gospel of John, in which we find that "life" (along with existence in its entirety) has come into being through the Word (*All things came into being through it* [the Word], *and without it not one thing came into being. What has come into being in it was life* ... 1:3-4a). We also find that the life brought into being in the Word has served as a light to all people (... *and the life was the light to all people.* 1:4b). Then, to illustrate this point, the author tells us that John (the Baptist) was sent by God, to testify to the light: *There was a man sent from God, whose name was John. He came as a witness to testify to the light. He himself was not the light, but he came to testify to the light.* (1:8). Later, in the main narrative, Jesus makes it clear that, in testifying to the light, John had testified to the truth ("*You*

sent messengers to John, and he testified to the truth."
5:33).

The believer's obligation to testify to the truth is
expressed more directly by the author of the Gospel (or
perhaps John the Baptist) in verses 3:31-34:

> *The one who comes from above is above all; the*
> *one who is of the earth belongs to the earth and*
> *speaks about earthly things. The one who comes*
> *from heaven is above all. He testifies to what he*
> *has seen and heard, yet no one accepts his*
> *testimony. Whoever has accepted his testimony*
> *has certified this, that God is true. He whom God*
> *has sent speaks the words of God, for he gives the*
> *Spirit without measure.* (3:31-34).

This passage applies to the one, *anyone*, who comes from
above, anyone who has seen and heard from God. Not
surprisingly, throughout the Gospel, many individuals are
portrayed as testifying to the truth: John the Baptist,
Jesus, colleagues of Jesus, the one who comes from
above, the man born blind, Lazarus, the author of the
Gospel, and the final editors of the Gospel.

Late in the Gospel - during his first appearance to his
male disciples[54] after his death - Jesus sends his disciples
to testify to the truth, as he had been sent (... *Jesus came*
and stood among them and said, "Peace be with you."...

---

[54] Mary Magdalene had already seen and spoken with Jesus, and had
been sent to testify to his brothers that Jesus was ascending to his
Father and theirs, his God, and theirs (verses 20:17b-18).

*Then the disciples rejoiced when they saw the Lord.
Jesus said to them again, "Peace be with you. <u>As the
Father has sent me, so I send you.</u>" 20:19-21).* And
finally, in case Peter isn't clear on what he is to do, Jesus
asks Peter, "do you love me." Each time Peter answers
that he does love Jesus, and Jesus immediately tells him,
"Feed my lambs" (or, equivalently "Tend my sheep" or
"Feed my sheep"). Each of these expressions is a
figurative way of saying "testify to the truth" to those who
might be receptive to the truth.

> *When they had finished breakfast, Jesus said to
> Simon Peter, "Simon son of John, do you love me
> more than these[55]?" He [Simon] said to him,
> "Yes, Lord; you know that I love you." <u>Jesus said
> to him, "Feed my lambs."</u> A second time he said
> to him, "Simon son of John, do you love me?" He
> said to him, "Yes, Lord; you know that I love you.
> <u>Jesus said to him, "Tend my sheep."</u> He said to
> him the third time, "Simon son of John, do you
> love me?" Peter felt hurt because he said to him
> for the third time, "Do you love me?" And he said
> to him, Lord, you know everything; you know that*

---

[55] Jesus' question here is somewhat ambiguous. Is he asking Peter if
Peter loves him more than these (the other disciples) love him? Or is
he asking if Peter loves him more than he (Peter) loves the other
disciples? I'm not sure, but the ambiguity is not important because in
subsequent repetitions of his question, Jesus omits the "more than
these," and the immediate and larger context does not depend on
either a comparison of Peter's love to that of other disciples *or* on
Peter's love of the other disciples.

I love you." Jesus said to him, "Feed my sheep."
(21:15-17).

From beginning to end, the Gospel stresses the
importance of testifying. The believer's testimony to the
truth is intended to bring others to "life" (eternal life), a
state of being in which they will participate in realizing
the purpose behind existence: the bringing of love into
being in this otherwise merely material, and hence
meaningless, world.

Why Was (and Is) Testifying Necessary?

Testimony to the truth was necessary in Jesus' day (as
in ours) because of widespread misunderstandings and
misrepresentations of the truth - and the evils they lead to.
Some of these misunderstandings, misrepresentations, and
evils are identified within the Gospel, and they can be
thought of as the Gospel's critique of the world.

Before we address this critique, I believe a word of
caution is in order. The Gospel speaks from within its
immediate context: ancient Judea under Roman rule. In
this context the critique inevitably addresses flaws in the
existing Jewish community and religious institutions
under Roman governance. Some readers of the Gospel
might mistakenly see the Gospel's critique as being aimed
at the Judaism of that time, and by extension at Judaism
today. Some have seen the Gospel as an anti-Semitic text,
and have employed the Gospel for anti-semitic purposes.

These views and uses of the Gospel are mistaken, and frankly represent an anti-Gospel. The problem is never other people and what they are doing. The real problem is always much closer to home than that. And finally, whatever flaws might have existed in Judaism in Jesus' day remain with us in all religions and social institutions today.

The basic charge against certain Jews and Jewish authorities in the Gospel of John is not that they are Jewish, but rather that they are too worldly. The critique of certain Jews and Jewish authorities in the Gospel is merely a particular instance of the Gospel's larger critique of "the world." This larger critique was warranted in Jesus' time and place, and it applies to the world we occupy today.

The Gospel's Critique of the World

The first indication of a fundamental problem in the world appears early in prologue when the author tells us, *The light shines in the darkness, and the darkness did not overcome it.* (1:5). What was, and is, this darkness? Clearly the darkness is opposed to, and/or stands in the way of, the light. The light is provided by the life (eternal life) that has come into being in response to the Word, in response to the truth. Both the light and the darkness were present during Jesus' lifetime, and during the time in which the Gospel was being written (the light shines in the darkness). And, as they are defined in the Gospel, they are with us today.

To be a follower of Jesus, that is, to believe and to embody the truth to which he testified, is to embody the light, and no longer walk in darkness (*Again Jesus spoke to them* [those who had been present at the "trial" of the woman caught in adultery], *saying, "I am the light of the world. Whoever follows me will never walk in darkness but will have the light of life."* 8:12).

The light is constituted by the truth; the darkness (as represented in the Gospel) is constituted by ignorance, false glory (looking for glory in all the wrong places), fear, hatred, violence (sacred and secular), lies and murder.

Ignorance

The Greek word translated in verse 1:5 as "overcome" could also be translated as "comprehend." Either way, or both ways, it makes sense in the context of the Gospel. Understood as "overcome," the word suggests active opposition to the light; understood as "comprehend," the word suggests simply a lack of understanding of the light, or of the truth which constitutes the light. Thus, the author of the Gospel is able to tell us,

> *He* [Jesus, the true light, the truth] *was in the world, and the world came into being through him; yet the world did not know him. He came to*

his own, and his own people did not accept him.
(1:10-11).

And Jesus is able to tell his listeners,

"If you love me, you will keep my commandments. And I will ask the Father, and he will give you another Advocate, to be with you forever. This is the Spirit of truth, whom <u>the world cannot receive because it neither sees nor knows him.</u>" (14:15-17), and

"Righteous Father, <u>the world does not know you,</u> but I know you; and these know that you have sent me." (17:25).

False glory

Jesus understood that seeking glory from human beings rather than from God stood in the way of people's ability to recognize and accept the truth to which he was testifying. As he put it to some listeners who did not believe him,

"I do not accept glory from human beings. But I know that you do not have the love of God in you. ... <u>How can you believe when you accept glory from one another and do not seek the glory that comes from the one who alone is God.</u>" (5:41-44).

Jesus also spoke out against people who sought glory for themselves: *"<u>Those who speak on their own seek their own glory;</u> but the one who seeks the glory of him who*

243

sent him is true, and there is nothing false in him."(7:18) Some, even among the authorities believed what Jesus was teaching, but were afraid to speak out because of their love of human glory. As the author of the Gospel puts it: ... *many, even of the authorities, believed in him. But because of the Pharisees they did not confess it, for fear that they would be put out of the synagogue; for they loved human glory more than the glory that comes from God.* (12:42-43).

Fear

In verses 12:42-43 we find that fear, in addition to love of human glory, stands in the way of people's willingness to testify to the truth, even if they believe. A more dramatic portrayal of the role of fear is implied in Peter's three-fold denial that he knows Jesus. The stage for the denial is set when Jesus, in reference to his coming death and resurrection, tells Peter, *"Where I am going, you cannot follow me now; but you will follow afterward."* (13:36). When Peter objects, volunteering to lay down his life so that he can follow now, Jesus answers, *"Will you lay down your life for me? Very truly, I tell you, before the cock crows, you will have denied me three times."* (13:38). The first denial comes when, after Jesus has been arrested, a woman who is guarding the gate to the courtyard of Caiaphas, asks Peter, *"You are not also one of this man's disciples, are you?,"* and Peter answers, *"I am not."* (18:17). The second denial occurs, while Jesus is being questioned by Caiaphas, and Peter is asked by the slaves and temple police, *"You are not also one of his disciples, are you?, and again Peter replies, "I am not."* (18:25). And the third comes when one of the slaves asks Peter, *"Did I not see you in the garden with him* [Jesus]*?"* (8:26). When Peter denies having been in the garden, the cock crows.

Hatred

The Gospel tells us that people who do evil hate the light because it might expose their evil doing. As Jesus (or the author of the Gospel) put it,

> *And this is the judgment, that the light has come into the world, and <u>people loved darkness rather than the light because their deeds were evil.</u> <u>For all who do evil hate the light</u> and do not come to the light so that their deeds may not be exposed. But those who do what is true come to the light, so that it may be clearly seen that their deeds have been done in God.* (3:19-21).

Jesus refers to hatred again when he tells his brothers (who have urged him to go to Judea to testify in public in spite of the danger), *"My time has not yet come, but your time is always here. The <u>world cannot hate you, but it hates me because I testify against it that its works are evil.</u>"* (7:7).

In any case, later in the Gospel, Jesus tells his disciples,

> *"If the world hates you, be aware that it hated me*
> *before it hated you. If you belonged to the world,*
> *the world would love you as its own. Because you*
> *do not belong to the world, but I have chosen you*
> *out of the world - therefore the world hates you."*
> (15:18-19).

The choosing to which Jesus refers in this passage is not
pre-determined or arbitrary. Jesus "chose" his disciples
by testifying to the truth, by giving them the word of God,
and letting them choose themselves according to their
response to the truth. In his intercessory prayer on behalf
of his disciples, Jesus reports to the Father, *"I have given*
them your word, and the world has hated them because
they do not belong to the world, just as I do not belong to
the world." (17:14). The world hates those who do not
belong to the world, those who belong to the truth.

Sacred violence

The world, inasmuch as it is not in accord with the
truth, is prone to violence and persecution, some of the
most notorious examples of which are perpetrated in the
name of religion. Thus, the scribes and Pharisees are
under the impression that stoning a woman caught in
adultery is appropriate because it is called for in the law
of Moses: *The scribes and the Pharisees brought a*
woman who had been caught in adultery; and making her
stand before all of them, they said to him, "Teacher, this
woman was caught in the very act of committing adultery.
Now in the law Moses commanded us to stone such

women. Now what do you say?" (8:3-5). Plans to kill Jesus are also justified with reference to violations of the law. Having successfully invited a man who could not walk to pick up his mat and walk on the sabbath, Jesus is persecuted by his fellow Jews for violating the law: *Therefore the Jews started persecuting Jesus, because he was doing such things on the sabbath.* (5:16). And when Jesus tells his accusers, *"My Father is still working, and I also am working"* (5:17), his accusers seek to kill him (*For this reason the Jews were seeking all the more to kill him, because he was not only breaking the sabbath, but was calling God his own Father, thereby making himself equal to God.* (5:18, see also verses 7:1 and 7:19). Of course, Jesus was not making himself equal to God. To be a child of God is to have come to believe the truth and to have endeavored to bring one's will and behavior into accord with the truth.

Secular violence

Although there was considerable resistance to Jesus and his message among his people, Jesus apparently did attract many followers. After his success in raising Lazarus from the "dead" the author of the Gospel tells us, *Many of the Jews therefore, who had come with Mary* [a sister of Lazarus] *and had seen what Jesus did, believed in him. But some of them went to the Pharisees and told them what he had done.* (11:45-46). Jesus' success in attracting a following alarmed the chief priests and Pharisees, who convened a council and said, *"What are we to do? ... This man is performing many signs. If we*

let him go on like this. Everyone will believe in him, and
the Romans will come and destroy both our holy place
and our nation." (11:47-48). What *are* they to do? The
author of the Gospel tells us that Caiaphas, the high priest,
had a plan:

> *But one of them, Caiaphas, who was high priest*
> *that year, said to them, "You know nothing at all!*
> *You do not understand that it is better for you to*
> *have one man die for the people than to have the*
> *whole nation destroyed."* (11:49-50).

The author then adds,

> *He did not say this on his own, but being high*
> *priest that year he prophesied that Jesus was*
> *about to die for the nation, and not for the nation*
> *only, but to gather into one the dispersed children*
> *of God. So from that day on they planned to put*
> *him to death.* (11:49-53).

Caiaphas may have "prophesied" that Jesus was about
to die, but he wasn't willing to leave Jesus' death to God
or chance. Caiaphas arranges for Jesus to be arrested and
brought before Pilate on political charges in order to force
Pilate to sentence Jesus to death. Thus, at his
arraignment, Pilate asks Jesus, *"Are you the king of the*
Jews?" (18:33b). When he finds out that Jesus' kingdom
is not of this world, but rather about something as
insubstantial as "the truth," Pilate declares, *"I find no*
case against him." (18:38). Nevertheless he has Jesus
flogged and crowned with thorns and dressed in a purple

robe. This does not satisfy the crowd which persists in calling for Jesus' death for claiming to be the Son of God. The argument that finally works however is not theological but rather political; they point out to Pilate that he will be in trouble if he releases Jesus:

> *From then on, Pilate tried to release him, but the Jews* [those under the influence of the religious authorities] *cried out, "If you release this man, you are no friend of the emperor. Everyone who claims to be a king sets himself against the emperor.* (19:12).

While "the world" is comfortable with violence, and in fact sponsors and sanctions violence for practical purposes (e.g., protecting a religious or political institution and, not incidentally, one's place in it), there is no place for violence in Jesus' kingdom. As Jesus puts it, in the Gospel of John, *"My kingdom is not from this world. If my kingdom were from this world, my followers would be fighting to keep me from being handed over to the Jews. But as it is, my kingdom is not from here."* (18:36).

Lies and murder

The issue of paternity arises again when Jesus tells some Jews who had once believed in him, but apparently no longer did , *"If you continue in my word you are truly my disciples; and you will know the truth, and the truth will make you free"* (8:31). His listeners object, saying, *"We are the descendants of Abraham and have never been slaves to anyone. What do you mean by saying, 'You will be made free'?"* (8:33). Jesus answers that everyone who commits sin is a slave to sin, " and then adds, *"I know that you are descendants of Abraham; yet you look for an opportunity to kill me, because there is no place in you for my word."* (8:37). After his listeners insist, *"Abraham is our father"* (8:39a), Jesus offers his perspective on their paternity:

> *"If you were Abraham's children, you would be doing what Abraham did, but now you are trying to kill me, a man who has told you the truth that I heard from God. This is not what Abraham did. You are indeed doing what your father does."* ... *"Why do you not understand what I say?" It is because you cannot accept my word. <u>You are from your father the devil</u>, and you choose to do your father's desires. <u>He was a murderer from the beginning and does not stand in the truth, because there is no truth in him. When he lies, he speaks according to his own nature, for he is a liar and the father of lies.</u>"* (8:39b-44).

Jesus' critique of those who were attempting to kill him in this passage applies to more than his immediate audience. Lies and murder have been with us from the beginning, and show no sign of ending. The fundamental lie here is that God's purpose (or, if you prefer, the purpose behind existence) can be served by violence.[56]

All of these sources of darkness get in the way of people coming to know the truth. Testifying to the truth is necessary in order to counteract these, and other, sources of darkness and to bring people to life (eternal life) so that they can participate in bringing love into being, and thereby realizing the purpose behind existence.

How We Can Testify

Testimony to the truth can given both verbally, by speaking or writing the truth, and non-verbally, by performing acts of love. In the Gospel of John, Jesus testifies primarily by speaking the truth. But he also testifies in his willingness to lay down his life in order to make the truth known. People sometimes speak of the need to "speak truth to power,"[57] i.e., to bear witness to the truth to those who have power over us. Jesus spoke the truth to power in his encounter with Pontius Pilate:

---

[56] A further discussion of sacred violence, violence perpetrated in the name of religion, is beyond the scope of this book. However for anyone interested in the topic I highly recommend *Violence and the Sacred*, by Rene Girard, translated by Patrick Gregory, Johns Hopkins Press, 1977.

[57] "This phrase originated with the Quakers in a 1955 pamphlet (Speak Truth to Power: A Quaker Search for an Alternative to Violence) promoting pacifism, in the belief that love can overcome hatred. It has come to mean "speaking out to those in authority" and is now used in politics and human rights activism." Urban Dictionary (www.urbandictionary.com), November 3, 2013.

Pilate therefore said to him, <u>"Do you refuse to</u>
<u>speak to me? Do you not know that I have the</u>
<u>power to release you, and the power to crucify</u>
<u>you?"</u> Jesus answered him, "You would have no
power over me unless it had been given you from
above ..." (19:10).

We too could be called to speak the truth to power.
But most often we will be called to speak truth when all
that we risk is our social or economic standing.
Moreover, the truth we need to speak does not need to be
a top-down critique of the world. Most often we only
need to address an immediate situation, and nudge things
in the direction of love and truth.

It's possible to testify to the truth in any situation, no
matter how unpromising or how dire. Anne Frank is said
to have put it this way, "How wonderful it is that nobody
needs to wait a single moment before starting to improve
the world."

Inasmuch as we believe the truth, love others (all
others, and unconditionally), and testify to the truth, we
have eternal life and play a constructive part in realizing
the purpose behind existence. When the Gospel first
speaks of God having sent the Son so that people might
have eternal life (in verse 3:16), it immediately follows up
by saying that God sent the Son not to condemn the
world, but in order that the world might be *saved* through
him. We will address the meaning of salvation in the next
chapter.

Points to Keep in Mind

- To believe the truth is to recognize our personal responsibility to testify to the truth.

- By testifying to the truth we recruit others for the purpose of bringing love into being in this otherwise merely material world.

- We testify to the truth (or fail to do so) in everything that we say and do.

- It is possible to testify to the truth in any and all circumstances in which we find ourselves.

Chapter 11

SALVATION

"For God so loved the world that he gave his only Son, so that everyone who believes in him may not perish but may have eternal life. Indeed, God did not send the Son into the world to condemn the world, but in order that the world might be saved through him." (3:16-17)

So far we have established an understanding of who God is, who we are, and what we are meant to be doing - as these elements of the truth are represented in the Gospel of John. All that remains to be done in order to complete our quest for the truth to which Jesus testified is to establish what salvation is - as it is represented in the Gospel of John.

Salvation is mentioned first in Chapter 3 of the Gospel, at the end of (or just after) the conversation between Jesus and Nicodemus. In this conversation Jesus tells Nicodemus (or the author of the Gospel tells the reader), *"Indeed, God did not send the Son into the world to condemn the world, but <u>in order that the world might be saved through him.</u>"* (3:17). In this verse we are told that God's purpose in sending the Son was to save the world. This understanding is confirmed in the Gospel when Jesus tells his listeners: *"I do not judge anyone who hears my words and does not keep them, for <u>I came not to</u>*

judge the world, but to save the world. " (12:47). The focus of salvation is then narrowed from salvation of *the world* to salvation of *an individual* in "the good shepherd discourse"[58] (verses 10:1-18). In this talk Jesus declares that those who enter "the sheepfold" by him will be saved (*I am the gate. Whoever enters by me will be saved, and will come in and go out and find pasture.* " 10:9).

Salvation is a major concern of the Gospel of John, but what did the author (and Jesus, as he is represented in the Gospel) mean by salvation? How and when do individuals come to be saved? *From* what, and *to* what, is the individual saved? And how, and in what sense, is the world to be saved? In order to find answers to these and related questions, we will examine the passages in the Gospel that explicitly mention salvation and determine their meaning in the context of the Gospel as a whole.

How and When

In verse 3:17 of the Gospel (*"Indeed, God did not send the Son into the world to condemn the world, but in order that the world might be saved through him.* ") we are told that the world is to be saved through the Son *and* that to be saved is to not be condemned. Verse 3:18 then

---

[58] The titles I have given to the various discourses (talks), here and elsewhere, are derived from the subject matter of portions of the text. The titles are similar to but not identical with those found in The New Oxford Annotated Bible with The Aprocrypha: An Ecumenical Study Bible, Completely Revised and Enlarged, Oxford University Press, 1991.

shifts the focus from salvation (non-condemnation) of the world to salvation (non-condemnation) of individuals, and links individual salvation to belief (*"Those who believe in him (the Son) are not condemned; but those who do not believe are condemned already, because they have not believed* in the name of the only Son of God" 3:18).

If we were to stop at verse 3:18, we might jump to the conclusion that belief is all that is necessary for salvation. But the Gospel continues, now linking condemnation and non-condemnation to what people *do*:

> *And this is the judgment, that the light has come into the world, and people loved darkness rather than light because their deeds were evil. For all who do evil hate the light and do not come to the light, so that their deeds may not be exposed. But those who do what is true come to the light, so that it may be clearly seen that their deeds have been done in God.:* (3:19-21).

The NRSV translation of this passage speaks of "judgment" rather than "condemnation," but this is a distinction without a difference. In the NRSV translation, the same Greek word is translated sometimes as judgment, sometimes as condemnation. They mean the same thing in the Gospel of John. The important point in this passage is that judgment/condemnation befalls people who "do evil." And, although the text doesn't explicitly say so, we can read between the lines to see that salvation - freedom from judgment/condemnation - comes to those

who believe *and* "do what is true." The final verse of our
passage equates doing "what is true" with doing "in God,"
i.e., while abiding in God.

Salvation and eternal life

To be or to act *in* God (verses 3:19-21) is language
that is associated elsewhere in the Gospel with eternal
life. A connection between salvation and eternal life is
also suggested by the parallels between verses 3:16 and
3:17. In verse 3:16 people's acceptance of Jesus'
testimony (their belief in him) leads to eternal life, but in
verse 3:17, their acceptance of his testimony (and thereby
entering into his being) leads to salvation of the world.
By placing these two verses next to each other, the author
of the Gospel is inviting the reader to think of eternal life
as in some way related to salvation.

Since what a person needs to do in order to be saved
(i.e., believing and doing what is true) is precisely what
he or she needs to do in order to have eternal life, we
might be inclined to conclude that eternal life *is* salvation,
or that one is saved *because* he or she has come to have
eternal life. However, I am inclined to think of salvation
and eternal life as distinct consequences of coming to
believe and doing what is true. In any case, a person is
saved by believing and doing what is true (loving others
and testifying to the truth). In doing what is true the
person participates directly in realizing the purpose
behind existence - the bringing of love into being in this
world.

A metaphorical representation of salvation

In the good shepherd discourse (10:1-18), to be saved is "to enter the sheepfold by the gate." Jesus first warns his listeners against people who do *not* enter the sheepfold by the gate: *"Very truly, I tell you, anyone who does not enter the sheepfold by the gate but climbs in by another way is a thief and a bandit."* 10:1). He goes on to say,

> *"The one who enters by the gate is the shepherd of the sheep. The gatekeeper opens the gate for him, and the sheep hear his voice. He calls his own sheep by name and leads them out. When he has brought out all his own, he goes ahead of them, and the sheep follow him because they know his voice."* (10:2-4).

In these verses, "the sheepfold" is salvation (and/or eternal life), "the shepherd of the sheep" is Jesus," "the gatekeeper" is God, "the gate" is the truth, and "his own sheep" are all those who follow the shepherd. They follow the shepherd because they know his voice, that is, because they recognize the truth of what he is saying. Jesus actually fills multiple roles in this material. He is also the gate inasmuch as he embodies and represents the truth through which one has access to eternal life. He is the shepherd inasmuch as he calls his own sheep by name and leads them out (of this world), and because the sheep follow him. He is also "the one who enters by the gate" inasmuch as he is "the shepherd of the sheep."

The full cast of characters:

- The sheepfold is (represents) salvation and eternal life
- The gatekeeper is God
- The gate is the truth/Jesus
- The shepherd/good shepherd is Jesus (and anyone who enters by the gate)
- One who enters by the gate is Jesus, and all believer/doers of the truth
- The sheep are all those who know (recognize) and follow the shepherd's voice

The multiplicity of roles that Jesus plays in the good shepherd discourse is similar to the multiplicity of roles that he claims for himself when - in response to Thomas' question, *"Lord, we do not know the way to where you are going. How can we know the way?"* (14:5) - he answers, *"I am the way, the truth, and the life. No one comes to the Father except through me."* (14:16) Jesus is "the way" inasmuch as one enters salvation/eternal life by following Jesus' example and entering into his being. He is "the truth" inasmuch as the truth constitutes his true and transcendent self. And he is "the life" (eternal life) inasmuch as to enter into Jesus' being is to enter into eternal life.

Individual salvation, in the here and now

Just as people come to have eternal life as individuals, people come to be saved as individuals. People are saved individually, rather than collectively, because every step of the process toward salvation is personal. A person senses that there is, or may be, such a thing as the truth. He or she listens for the truth; hears and comes to an understanding of the truth; recognizes that it *is* both true and *the* truth; adopts the truth as his or her own; and chooses to bring his or her life into accord with the truth. These are all inherently personal steps.

People are saved individually and, as was true of coming to have eternal life, they are saved in the here and now, during their otherwise ordinary lives in this, the material world. This is indicated in the good shepherd discourse, in which the entering of the sheepfold is spoken of primarily in the present tense:

> *"The gatekeeper opens the gate for him, and the sheep hear his voice. He calls his own sheep by name and leads them out* [of this world] (10:3),

> *"When he has brought out all his own, he goes ahead of them, and the sheep follow him because they know his voice."* (10:4), and

> *"I am the gate. Whoever enters by me will be saved, and will come in* [enter the sheepfold, be saved] *and go out and find pasture.* (10:9).

Verse 10:9 might seem to contradict the idea that salvation occurs in the here and now. The verse says that whoever enters *will* be saved, and *will* come in and go out. These are clearly future events, but not relative to the

time at which the person/sheep "enters by the gate"
(accepts and embraces the truth).

The passages that address salvation explicitly and
metaphorically support the idea that people are saved as
individuals, and that they are saved during their lives in
this world. Other, less explicit and less direct, evidence
bearing on these conclusions can be found in what the
Gospel tells us about resurrection, sanctification, and
glorification. These too are personal events. They too
happen to individuals, and they happen during the
individual's otherwise ordinary life in this world.

Resurrection

The noun, "resurrection." appears in only two
passages in the Gospel of John. In the first passage Jesus
speaks of "the resurrection of life" and the "resurrection
of condemnation." This is what he tells his listeners,

> *"Very truly, I tell you, <u>anyone who hears my word
> and believes him who sent me has eternal life, and
> does not come under judgment, but has passed
> from death to life</u>. Very truly, I tell you, <u>the hour
> is coming, and is now here</u>, when the dead will
> hear the voice of the Son of God, and those who
> hear will live. ... Do not be astonished at this; for
> the hour is coming when all who are in their
> graves <u>will hear</u> his voice and <u>will come out</u> -
> those who have done good, to the resurrection of*

*life, and those who have done evil, to the
resurrection of condemnation."* (5:24-29).

In the first sentence of this passage (verse 5:24), Jesus makes the point that those who hear his word and believe God *already* have eternal life, having already passed from death to life. More relevant to the topic of salvation, Jesus states that anyone who hears his word (the truth) and believes "does not come under judgment." To not come under judgment is an aspect of being saved, as that term is represented in verses 3:17-18. Thus, we can read verse 5:24 as saying that, the believer is *already saved* in the sense that he does not come under judgment. In the second sentence (verse 5:25), Jesus announces that the hour when this will happen *is now here.*

In the final two sentences (verses 5:28 and 29), Jesus states that the hour is coming when *all* who are in their graves will hear his voice, and that those who do good will come out to "the resurrection of life" (have eternal life and not be condemned) while those who *do evil* will come out to "the resurrection of condemnation" (i.e., will be condemned). In these verses, Jesus represents resurrection, coming to have life, and (indirectly) salvation as something that will happen in the future; however, this future resurrection will also be contemporaneous with (in the here and now of) the individual who comes to hear Jesus' word, believes, and does good.

The word " resurrection" appears again in the story of the raising of Lazarus (verses 11:1-44). In the conversation between Jesus and Martha (verses 11:21-27), Jesus attempts to console Martha, telling her that her brother, Lazarus, will rise again. Martha then replies, *"I know that he will rise again in the resurrection on the last day."* (verse 11:24). Rather than confirm Martha's understanding of a resurrection at some indefinite time in the future, Jesus replies, *"I am the resurrection, and the life. Those who believe in me, even though they die, will live, and everyone who lives and believes in me will never die. Do you believe me?"* (11:25-26). In his reply Jesus is saying that the resurrection is already present, and that he embodies and represents that resurrection. Having begun by speaking about himself ("I am ...") Jesus then speaks of those who live and believe in him, saying that, even thought they die (in the bodily sense), they will never die (in the transcendent sense). To Jesus, resurrection encompasses both salvation (non-condemnation) *and* eternal life, both of which come to an individual in the here and now.

Sanctification

In the Gospel of John, Jesus also speaks of people being "sanctified" (made holy). In the first instance, Jesus speaks of *himself* as having been sanctified during his defense against a charge of blasphemy (in verses 10:32-36, see Chapter 7). In that passage, Jesus identifies himself as "the one whom the Father has sanctified and

264

sent into the world." But Jesus did not see sanctification as applying only to himself. Later in the Gospel, during his prayer of intercession on their behalf, Jesus asks God to sanctify his disciples.:

> *"I have given them your word, and the world has hated them because they do not belong to the world, just as I do not belong to the world. ... Sanctify them in the truth; your word is truth. As you have sent me into the world, so I have sent them into the world. And for their sakes I sanctify myself, so that they also may be sanctified in truth."* (17:14-19).

This passage makes it clear that Jesus understood that his disciples (his followers) could, and would, be sanctified "in the truth." They would be sanctified "in the truth" (made holy) by coming to believe, and live their lives in accord with, the truth.

While Jesus speaks of himself as having been sanctified in his own lifetime ("I sanctify myself"), nothing in the explicit "sanctification passages" indicates when Jesus' followers would become sanctified. However, evidence that Jesus meant that his followers would be sanctified during their lives in this world (and how this would come about) can be found in the "vine and branches discourse" (verses 15:1-11).

In the vine and branches discourse, Jesus likens himself to "the true vine" and God to a vinegrower (*"I am the true vine, and my Father is the vinegrower."* 15:1).

Jesus invites his followers to think of him as "the true vine" through which the truth passes to and through his disciples. He then tells them that they are the branches (*"I am the vine, you are the branches."* 15:5), and explains how things work: *"He* [God, the Father] *removes every branch in me that bears no fruit. Every branch that bears fruit* [every true disciple] *he prunes to make it bear more fruit.* (15:2). He then tells his disciples, *"You have already been cleansed* [pruned[59]] *by the word that I have spoken to you."* (15:3). Jesus then tells his disciples to abide in him as he abides in them, for apart from him (apart from the truth that constituted Jesus' being) they can do nothing (*"Abide in me as I abide in you. Just as the branch cannot bear fruit by itself unless it abides in the vine, neither can you unless you abide in me."* (15:4)

Those branches (individuals) who *do* bear fruit (in themselves and in those around them) are pruned of residual thoughts, intentions, and behaviors that are not fruitful (that don't contribute to the bringing of love into being) through a continuing encounter with the truth. As we are pruned, we are sanctified/made holy. The pruning/sanctification saves us, and it contributes to saving those who depend on us for the truth. It is a process that occurs within a person, during his or her lifetime in this world.

---

[59] Curiously, the NRSV translators chose to translate the same Greek word that it had translated as "pruned" in verse 14:2 as "cleansed" in verse 15:3 Could the translators have been attempting to put some distance between Jesus and the believer?

Glorification

Glory and glorification are spoken of often, and throughout the Gospel of John - more often than are salvation, resurrection, or sanctification. And, unlike these other terms, glorification applies to God as well as to man.

Glory is first spoken of in the prologue to the Gospel: *And the Word was made flesh and lived among us, and we have seen his glory, the glory as of a father's only son, full of grace and truth.* (1:14). Here the reference is to Jesus as the Word made flesh, and the author of the Gospel is reminding his readers/hearers that they have been witnesses to Jesus' glory. Glory is mentioned next in the story of the changing of water into wine at the wedding in Cana (verses 2:1-11). The story ends with the author of the Gospel telling us, *Jesus did this, the first of his signs, in Cana of Galilee, and revealed his glory; and his disciples believed in him.* (2:11).

When Jesus himself addresses the subject of glory, it is to warn his listeners against accepting glory from other human beings rather than from God:

> *"I have come in my Father's name, and you do not accept me; if another comes in his own name, you will accept him. How can you believe when you accept glory from one another and do not seek the glory that comes from the one alone who is God?"* (5:43-44).

Our (or if you prefer, people's) tendency to seek glory from one another is cited in the Gospel to explain the failure of many who *did* believe to acknowledge that they did so. As the author of the Gospel puts it, *Nevertheless many, even of the authorities, believed in him. But because of the Pharisees they did not confess it, for fear that they would be put out of the synagogue; for they loved human glory more than the glory that comes from God.* 12:42-43).

Jesus also urged his listeners to seek *God's* glory rather than their own (*"Those who speak on their own seek their own glory; but the one who seeks the glory of him who sent him is true, and there is nothing false in him."* (7:18). God seeks Jesus' glory (*"... I do not seek my own glory; there is one who seeks it and he* [God] *is the judge."* 8:50). And our attempts to glorify ourselves will be in vain (*Jesus answered, "If I glorify myself, my glory is nothing. It is my Father who glorifies me ..."* 8:54).

We are not to seek glory *from* one another, nor are we to seek glory *for* ourselves, but the fact remains that the Son of Man *is* to be glorified (*Jesus answered them, "The hour has come for the Son of Man to be glorified."* 12:23). In fact, the Son and God are to be mutually glorified - God in the Son, and the Son in God:

When he had gone out [When Judas, the son of Simon Iscariot had departed, having been dismissed by Jesus], *Jesus said, "Now the Son of Man has been glorified, and*

God has been glorified in him." If God has been glorified in him, God will glorify him in himself and will glorify him at once. (13:31-32). Jesus was glorified not by Judas' departure, but rather by Jesus' willingness to face death in order to make the truth known.

The point that the Father is glorified in the Son, and the Son is glorified in the Father, is made again later, at the beginning of Jesus' prayer of intercession on behalf of his disciples: *After Jesus had spoken these words, he looked up to heaven and said, "Father, the hour has come; glorify your Son so that the Son may glorify you."* (17:1). The glorification of the Father comes about as a result of the things that the Son does, as is made clear just a few verses on: *"I glorified you on earth by finishing the work that you gave me to do."* (17:4).

The mutual glorification of God and Son applies to others as well as to Jesus. This point is made clear in the vine and branches discourse, when Jesus tells his followers, *"My Father is glorified by this, that you bear much fruit and become my disciples."* (15:8). Moreover, Jesus was glorified in his disciples, as can be seen when he tells the Father, *"All mine are yours, and all yours are mine; and I have been glorified in them."* 17:10). And the disciples were glorified in Jesus (*"The glory that you have given me, I have given them, ..."* 17:22). The mutual glorifications - the Son in God/God in the Son and Jesus in the disciples/the disciples in Jesus - are further indications that man and God are on an adventure together, and we will succeed or fail together.

In those passages in the Gospel that speak of glorification actually happening, glorification comes to an individual as a result of his or her own response to the truth, and it comes to the individual in the here and now.

Salvation, From and To

It may be helpful to think of salvation as involving the movement from one state of being to another. If so, then we could think of salvation as salvation *from* mortality (from material death being the final word about our lives) *to* immortality, eternal life in God. We could also think of salvation as salvation *from* condemnation (or, equivalently, negative judgment) *to* the resurrection of life, to sanctification and glorification.

Although it is not explicitly mentioned in the Gospel, we can think of salvation as salvation *from* meaninglessness *to* meaningfulness. The truth is that, apart from our participation in the bringing of love into being in this world nothing matters, nothing will have mattered when all is said and done. What does matter, what will have mattered, are our acts of divine (universal, unconditional) love, including our testimony to the truth. These acts directly contribute to realizing the purpose behind existence: the bringing of love into being in this, the otherwise merely material, world. To perform an act of love and testimony is to participate, whether we think of it as such or not, in the kingdom of God.

Salvation of the World

So far we have focused on how an individual person comes to be saved. But what about "the world"? Is the world (every*thing*) saved? Is every*one* saved? In what sense is the world to be saved?

It is clear that the author of the Gospel, and Jesus as represented therein, understood that the world was to be saved. God sent the Son *"in order that the world might be saved through him."* (3:17) and Jesus claims *"...I came not to judge the world, but to save the world."* (12:47). And, although it doesn't have quite the same weight, some Samaritans, having listened to Jesus' testimony, came to believe *"for we have heard for ourselves, and we know that this is truly the Savior of the world."* (4:42).

Did Jesus/the author of the Gospel believe that the world would be saved in the sense that *everything* or *everyone* in it would be saved? The understanding that every*one* will be saved is highly unlikely in the face of so many qualifications set on salvation and/or eternal life throughout the Gospel. In his good shepherd discourse, Jesus states not that everyone will be saved, but only those who enter by him, the gate (*"I am the gate. Whoever enters by me will be saved ..."* (10:9). From the beginning of the Gospel we find similar qualifications. In the prologue, we find that only those *who received Jesus, who believed in his name* were given power *to become children of God.* (1:12). And when Jesus declares, *"Do not be astonished at this; for the hour is coming when* all *who are in their graves will hear his voice and will come out - those who have done good, to the resurrection of life, and those who have done evil, to the resurrection of condemnation."* (5:28-29), he does not mean that all will be saved. Only "those who have done good" will come out to "the resurrection of life." Those who have done evil will come to "the resurrection of condemnation" (the opposite of salvation).

In chapter 6 of the Gospel, after his "bread of life discourse" (6:25-51), Jesus declares,

> *"And this is the will of him who sent me, that I should lose nothing* [none][60] *of all that* [whom] *he has sent me, but raise it* [them] *up on the last day. This is indeed the will of my Father, that all who see the Son and believe in him may have eternal life; and I will raise them up on the last day."* (6:39-40).

The point to be made here is that the "all" who are to be raised up does *not* encompass everyone, but rather, only those whom God has "sent" to Jesus, i.e., "all who see the Son and believe in him." To not be sent by God to Jesus is an after-the-fact designation. No one is pre-ordained or doomed to being lost.

Not everyone and everything in the world is to be saved. So, how is it, and in what sense, is the world to be

---

[60] In verse 6:39 I have taken the liberty to indicate, in square brackets, how I would have translated certain words to make its meaning consistent with its immediate and larger contexts in the Gospel.

saved? The answer that is compatible with all of the evidence, and the answer that I am inclined to believe, is that the world (the material world) is saved from meaninglessness inasmuch as it has served as the stage upon which love has come into being.

Points to Keep in Mind

- **Individuals are saved inasmuch as they have believed the truth, loved others (all others, unconditionally) and testified to the truth.**

- **To be saved is to be saved *from* bodily death being the final word about our lives *to* eternal life in God ("the resurrection of life").**

- **To be saved is to be saved *from* judgment/condemnation *to* sanctification and glorification.**

- **To be saved is to be saved *from* meaninglessness *to* meaningfulness.**

- **The world (existence in its entirety) is saved inasmuch as it has served as the stage upon which love has come into being.**

Chapter 12

THE TRUTH IS

We began our quest for the truth by considering some fundamental questions about existence: Is existence about something, or nothing? Is there a purpose behind existence? Will anything that we do in this world have mattered, when all is said and done? I then observed that a representation of the truth about existence - a representation of the truth that strikes me as both true, and as *the* truth - can be found in the Gospel of John.

In this final chapter I will briefly summarize the truth - as it is represented in the Gospel of John - and provide answers to the fundamental questions about existence that were raised in Chapter One. I will also make general observations about the truth and the implications of the truth for religious institutions in general and Christianity in particular, and for living in the world as we find it.

The Truth

The truth is that there *is* a purpose behind existence. The purpose is to bring love into being, to infuse us, and through us, this otherwise merely material world with divine love, and in so doing to save us and existence in its entirety from meaninglessness, from having been in vain.

That there is a purpose behind existence, and that this purpose is to bring love into being, is just part of the larger truth about existence. This larger truth - as it is represented in the Gospel of John - can be thought of in relation to four major topics: who (or what) God is, who we are, what we are meant to be doing, and salvation.

Who (or what) God Is

The nature and existence of God

The truth (aka the Word) *is* God - and has been so from the beginning. The truth constitutes God's being, and thus can be thought of as the "substance" of God. Inasmuch as there *is* a truth behind existence, God exists.

Because the truth constitutes God's being, God cannot say or do just anything - and still be God. He can speak and act only in accord with the truth. Thus, God is not arbitrary or capricious, not given to changes of mood or mind. God is constant; we can depend on God. Because the truth is God, we can come to know God by - and *only* by - coming to know the truth. There is nothing that we can, or need to, know about God beyond the truth.

The truth is transcendent. Its origin and continuing locus of being lies outside the material world, outside of space and time. Because the truth is transcendent, that there *is* a truth behind existence, and *what* that truth is, cannot be established on the basis of material facts and analysis. The truth can be grasped only subjectively, through our recognition of the truth when we hear it, and through our recognition of the workings of the truth within ourselves and others.

God's purpose

God's ultimate purpose - or, if you prefer, the purpose behind existence - is to bring divine love (universal and unconditional respect, caring, kindness, mercy, ...) into being in this world. At the same time, God means to bring us to eternal life and save us and the world from meaninglessness.

God's modus operandi

God/the truth works through people, individuals in this world, to realize his/its ultimate purpose, the bringing of love into being in this world. He/it does so by revealing the truth to individuals, sending them to testify to the truth, and telling them what to say. God also draws people to the truth and participates in their recognition of the truth and in their efforts to live in accord with the truth.

Alternatively, in order to avoid causal language which can invite fruitless speculation about predestination and free will, we could say that sometimes the truth dawns on people. We have no way of knowing to whom, or when, this will happen. These people recognize within the truth their personal responsibility to bring their lives into accord with the truth; and they do so through their acts of love and testimony. Behind events such as these, we might see the fingerprints of the truth, of God, in this world.

God does not operate in any other way. God does not send down floods, fires, or punishments on us in order to correct our behavior; nature takes care of all of these things. God does not preordain or control events in this world. And not everything that happens is an expression of God's will. God does have a plan to save us, and through us the world, but that plan is simply to reveal himself (i.e., the truth) to us and depend on us to do our part in bringing love into being.

The truth invites and enables us to become its (God's) agents in realizing the purpose behind existence, the bringing of love into being, the infusion of this otherwise merely material world with love. That God works through us to realize the purpose behind existence means that we - God and man - are in this together.

Who We Are

We are the intended recipients of "life" (eternal life), a transcendent state of being, a state of being in relation to God (to the truth). We come to have eternal life, or fail to do so, according to our response to the truth. Inasmuch as we believe - and strive to bring our lives into accord with - the truth, we have eternal life. In the process, we pass from "death" (separation from the truth) to "life"; we come out of our "graves" to the "resurrection of life." We come to have eternal life, if it happens, in the here and now, during our otherwise ordinary lives in this world.

Those who have come to have eternal life can be said to be "born of God" (or, equivalently, "born from above"). Inasmuch as we have eternal life we abide in God, and God abides in us (or, if you prefer, we abide in the truth, and the truth abides in us). To have eternal life is to know and be one with God. Inasmuch as we have eternal life we are immortal; even though our material selves will die, we will live on eternally in God. To have eternal life is to belong to the truth, to value love, not hate; peace, not violence; forgiveness, not condemnation; truth, not lies; openness, not secrecy, glory from God, not the world; glory for God; not for oneself.

In his testimony to the truth, Jesus introduced the expression, "the Son of Man," as a way of referring to himself and any person who has come to believe and embody the truth. Those who do so are Sons and Daughters of Man. The responsibility of a Son/Daughter of Man is to do what Jesus did: love others and, more generally, make of his life a testament to the truth.

In any case - whether we recognize and choose to embrace the truth or not - we are the message to which our life has testified. From this perspective, we might ask ourselves, what is the message to which *our* life has testified?

What We Are Meant to Be Doing

What we need to do in order to receive eternal life and, more importantly, contribute to realizing the purpose behind existence, is to: (1) believe, (2) love, and (3) testify to the truth.

Believing

In order to have eternal life and to contribute effectively to the bringing of love into being, we need to believe the truth. Otherwise we are unlikely to remain focused on the task in the face of difficulties and distractions. Coming to believe the truth involves (a) coming to an adequate understanding of the truth and (b) recognizing it as the ultimate truth about existence in its entirety and about our individual lives in particular.

Believing is not entirely voluntary. We cannot *decide to* believe the truth, we either believe the truth or we don't. What we *can* do is to take seriously our sense (if we have it) that existence is, or might be, about something, that there *is* a purpose to existence, and that what we do in this world *does* matter. We can also pursue knowledge of the truth wherever we sense that it might be found. We can listen for the truth with an open mind and heart, and attempt to make sense of what we hear - sort out the wheat from the chaff and establish priorities. These efforts will assist us in coming to an understanding of the truth, and put us in a position to *discover* whether we believe what we have come up with, or not. In the meantime, disbelief can be an appropriate posture. To not believe *mis*representations of the truth (and there are many) can be an important step on our path to the truth.

A reliable basis for believing the truth behind existence cannot be found in "signs" or in scripture, or in human testimony by themselves. The only reliable basis for believing is divine testimony: hearing the truth directly from God (or, equivalently, divine confirmation of the testimony of others). The testimony of others (e.g., of Jesus, or of the author of the Gospel of John) can trigger our recognition of what we have already received directly from God. In such instances, we "re-cognize" (re-know) the truth.

Believing is not enough, by itself, to bring us to eternal life, make of us effective agents of the truth, and secure our salvation. In fact, there is no such thing as believing "by itself." This is because to believe the truth is to believe that there are things one must actually *do*. Believing prepares us for what we need to do, and what we need to *do* is to love others and testify to the truth.

Loving

Our primary obligation under the truth is to love others. Moreover, our love for others is the sole indicator of true discipleship.

We are to love others as God loves and as Jesus loved: universally and unconditionally. We can begin by adopting God's attitude (love toward the entire world) and his purpose (the bringing of love into being in this world).

Our love for others is to encompass: not judging (love trumps everything), forgiveness, non-violence, respect for others without regard for their social standing, their value to us, or their religious/political affiliation. It also includes a willingness to die, literally and/or figuratively if necessary, in order to bring the truth to others.

Testifying

To believe the truth is to be "sent" to testify to the truth, to recognize our personal responsibility to make the truth known. By testifying to the truth we recruit others for the task of bringing love into being in this world.

We testify to the truth (or fail to do so) in everything that we say and do. Our life - what we think, say and do - is our testimony. The good news is that it is possible to testify to the truth in whatever circumstances we find ourselves: rich or poor, educated or uneducated, sick or well, young or old, imprisoned or free. Acts of love testify to the truth, just as testifying is an act of love.

Salvation

To bring our lives - our intentions, words, and behavior - into accord with the truth is to be saved. We are saved *from* what would otherwise be the finality of death *to* eternal life. We are saved *from* judgment and condemnation *to* sanctification and mutual glorification. We are saved *from* meaninglessness, from having lived a meaningless life, *to* meaningfulness, to having contributed to the bringing of love into being in this world.

The *world* (material existence in its entirety) is saved from meaninglessness inasmuch as it has been the stage upon which love has come into being.

The truth in hand, we are now prepared to answer the fundamental questions about existence.

Questions and Answers

Is existence about something, or nothing? And, if something, *what* is existence about?

For existence to be "about" something, there would need to be a something with reference to which everything else can be understood to have meaning (or the absence thereof). In our present context, "the truth" could be that something. Everything in existence can be understood in relation to the truth - as playing a part in making the truth known and fulfilling its purpose, or in obscuring or misrepresenting the truth and thwarting its purpose). However, there is something else, something *within* the truth that I believe to be a better candidate. There is one thing within the truth to which everything else points and can be understood as meaningful, and that one thing is love. Love is the purpose behind existence and the end toward which the truth calls us.

So, yes. Existence *is* about something. Existence is about the bringing of love into being - the infusion of this otherwise merely material, and thus meaningless, world with divine love. It's as if love is all we need.[61]

Is there a purpose behind existence? And if there is, what is that purpose?

Yes. The purpose behind existence is to bring love into being *and* in so doing to save us - and existence in its entirety - from meaninglessness.

Does anything we do in this world really matter? Will anything have mattered when all is said and done? And, if so what is it that will have mattered?

Yes, what we do in this world does matter. What matters - what will be seen to have mattered when all is said and done - are our works of love and testimony to the truth, everything we do that is an expression of divine love.

---

[61] "There's nothing you can do that can't be done, Nothing you can sing that can't be sung. ... Nothing you can know that isn't known, Nothing you can see that isn't shown, Nowhere you can be that isn't where you're meant to be, It's easy. All you need is love, All you need is love, All you need is love, Love is all you need." From "All You Need Is Love," written by Gary Glitter, Paul McCartney, Mike Leander, and John Lennon, Copyright: Sony/ATV Tunes LLC, MCA Music Limited; Copyright 2000-2014 AZLyrics.com.

Observations and Implications

The truth is universal

Although we have found the truth in what is often thought of as a Christian document, the truth itself is not particularly Christian. The truth does not require or make explicit reference to Jesus or to Christianity. This is not surprising inasmuch as the truth existed from the beginning, before any person, religious institution existed.

Not only is the truth not particularly Christian, but Christianity is not particularly concerned with the truth to which Jesus testified. Christianity, as defined in its formal creeds and doctrines, is more concerned with its own message about Jesus - the circumstances of his birth, his relationship to God, his crucifixion and resurrection, and what he can be expected to do at some indefinite time in the future - than it is with Jesus' message about the truth. As a result, a person can think of him or herself as being a Christian without believing the truth to which Jesus testified - in fact, without even knowing that Jesus had come to tell us something.

A person need not think of him or herself as a Christian in order to come to understand, believe and choose to bring his or her life into accord with the truth. However, if a person *does* so he or she will be *in effect* recognizing Jesus as a, if not *the* messiah/christ, a person designated by God to advance his purpose in this world.

The truth is universal, applicable to all and accessible by all. It can be recognized and adopted by anyone whatever their current religious affiliation or lack thereof.

The truth does not belong to anyone

The truth does not belong to any person or institution. The best a person or institution can hope for is to belong to the truth, i.e., be drawn to, understand, and recognize the truth as the truth behind existence. Moreover, no person, group, culture, nationality, religious or other institution occupies a privileged position with respect to the truth. All stand in judgment before (are judged by) the truth.

Any religious (or other) institution *could* adopt the truth as the basis for its message and activities. To do so, the institution would need to: (1) make the proclamation of the truth its guiding purpose; (2) review its scripture, doctrines, liturgies, rituals, and underlying theology for compatibility with, and effective expression of, the truth; (3) edit or reinterpret material that does not effectively express the truth to ensure that what remains does so; and (4) encourage and support its members' efforts to understand and bring their lives into accord with the truth.

We need not wait for institutional change

Fortunately, we don't need to wait for institutional changes to happen. We can, as individuals, adopt the truth as our own, and in doing so enter into the informal fellowship of "people of good will" everywhere, i.e., those who believe that they are called to love others - all others and unconditionally - and to testify to the truth.

We can adopt the truth as our own whatever our present circumstances might be. We don't need to be well-educated, well to do, or well-connected. Our gender, race, ethnicity, religious affiliation or lack thereof, and our past do not matter. We can adopt God's attitude and purpose as our own. And we can begin today to commit acts of love for others and to testify to the truth.

We could start by taking stock of how we are behaving in our relationships with others in our families, jobs, and communities - and ask ourselves if our behavior expresses divine love for others and testifies to the truth. Or, less methodically, we could just go out and do one good thing after another.

The truth is not for sissies

At first glance, the truth to which Jesus testified, and the demands it places on us, may seem fairly mild. We might even ask, "Is that all there is?" In fact the truth *is not* particularly challenging - unless it is taken seriously.

To actually love indiscriminately and to speak the truth can upset the social equilibrium at every level of our lives - from personal relationships to business, politics, and religion. To love indiscriminately and speak the truth is highly subversive. I think of it as the "universal solvent" for social structures and ideologies that are abusive to humanity. Needless to say, people in positions of power may not appreciate having the structures and ideologies that sustain them dissolved.

Jesus took the truth seriously. He loved and testified to the truth, and was arrested and executed for his efforts. On occasion we may need to do something momentous, such as speaking the truth to Pontius Pilate, or to an investigative or congressional committee, in order to make the truth known. Most often we will not need to risk death (literal death) or imprisonment in order to testify to the truth. Often what will be at stake is social disapproval or economic loss.

We can love and testify simply by expressing our concern and respect for others; speaking kindly to the people we meet during our day, encouraging others in their good works, and contributing our time or resources to activities that serve the less fortunate. We can also take care of our own physical and mental health (put on *our* own oxygen masks first) so that we are in a position to help others when they need it. These are things that can be done on a daily - a moment by moment - basis, things that will contribute to the bringing of love into being, and saving ourselves and the world from meaninglessness.

~~~

In closing, I wish to make it clear that I believe that the truth to which Jesus testified - as it is represented in the Gospel of John - is both true and *the* truth about existence in its entirety and about our lives in particular.

What began with curiosity about "what Jesus' life was really about" has ended with understanding and belief. In particularly, I believe is that there is a purpose behind existence; that this purpose is to bring love into being - to infuse this world with divine love; that if I listen for, and am open to, the truth, it will come to me and remain with me; and if I love others - all others and indiscriminately - and testify to the truth, I will have contributed to bringing love into being, and my life will have mattered.

Thank you for following this effort to unearth the truth to which Jesus testified (or, for being sufficiently interested to skip to the end and read the conclusions). I hope that what I have done is sufficiently transparent that you will be able to identify and correct any mistakes and unfortunate choices of wording that I have made that stand in the way of your coming to understand and recognize the truth.

Acknowledgements

I have been encouraged and sustained throughout the process of writing this book by my wife, Sandra K. Schaefer. Sandy stood by me, brought home the bacon, and let me know when my writing wasn't up to snuff. Sandy was also was the final editor of this book.

Although their support hasn't always been explicit, I have always known that our two sons, Erich and Max Schaefer, supported me - whatever I was doing. In fact, when I wondered if I would live long enough to finish the book, Erich said, "Don't worry, Dad, we'll finish it for you." This hasn't proven necessary. However, Erich did provide the book's cover design and photograph (mosaic on ceiling of the Arian Baptistry in Ravenna, Italy).

My education on theological matters began at the University of San Francisco, where I was welcomed as a prodigal son by Father Joseph F. Eagan, S.J., then chairman of the theology department. While at USF, I benefited particularly from courses in exegetical methods taught by John H. Elliott, Professor Emeritus of Theology and Religious Studies; Biblical Greek taught by Father Arthur Swain; and from encouragement by Sister Mary Neal.

Many years ago, Jon Winokur invited me to write a book on anything that I might be interested in for his imprint with Viking/Penguin Press. When it became clear

291

that the topic I had in mind was too heavy for his imprint, Jon offered to help me connect me with the right people when I was ready to publish. Just the thought that I might have an avenue for publishing was a comfort along the way. Karl Greenfeld and others too have casually suggested that they would help me get published, leaving me in the embarrassing position of having several potential publishers but no book! This pressure proved helpful too.

Carroll and John Lewis read and provided constructive comments on early chapters of the *The Truth Is*. I also received comments and encouragement from Dale Rice, Tom Calcaterra, Orv Teising, Lise Lawson, and others. Their encouraging words led me to believe that I did have an audience.

www.ingramcontent.com/pod-product-compliance
Lightning Source LLC
Chambersburg PA
CBHW051722040426
42447CB00008B/923